SEVEN DAYS ON THE ROADS OF FRANCE

JUNE 1940

St Vladimir's Seminary Press

ORTHODOX CHRISTAN PROFILES SERIES

Number 2

The Orthodox Christian Profiles Series acquaints the reader on an intimate level with Orthodox figures that have shaped the direction of the Orthodox Church in areas of mission, ascetical and liturgical theology, scholarly and pastoral endeavors, and various other professional disciplines. The people featured in the series are mostly our contemporaries and most remain active in shaping the life of the Church today. A few will have fallen asleep in the Lord, but their influence remains strong and worthy of historical record. The mission of this series is to introduce inspirational Orthodox Christian leaders in various ministries and callings that build up the Body of Christ.

Chad Hatfield
Series Editor

Seven Days on the Roads of France

JUNE 1940

Vladimir Lossky

Edited by Nicholas Lossky

Translated by Michael Donley

ST VLADIMIR'S SEMINARY PRESS
YONKERS, NEW YORK 10707
2012

Library of Congress Cataloging-in-Publication Data

Lossky, Vladimir, 1903–1958.
   [Sept jours dans les routes de France, Juin 1940. English]
   Seven days on the roads of France, June 1940 / Vladimir Lossky ; edited by Nicholas
Lossky ; translated by Michael Donley.
      p. cm. — (Orthodox Christian profiles series ; no. 2)
     ISBN 978-0-88141-418-9
     1. Lossky, Vladimir, 1903–1958. 2. World War, 1939–1945—Personal narratives,
French. 3. World War, 1939–1945—Campaigns, France. 2. World War,
1939–1945—Refugees—France—Biography. 5. Theologians—France—Biography.
I. Lossky, Nicolas. II. Title.

D811.5.L62A3 2012
940.53'44092—dc23
[B]
                                  2012020881

Originally published in France under the title
Sept jours dans les routes de France, Juin 1940
Copyright © 1998
Éditions du Cerf
English version by permission.

TRANSLATION COPYRIGHT © 2012

ST VLADIMIR'S SEMINARY PRESS
575 Scarsdale Rd, Yonkers, NY 10707
1-800-204-2665
www.svspress.com

ISBN 978-0-88141-418-9

PRINTED IN THE UNITED STATES OF AMERICA

In memoriam

Elizabeth Obolensky (née Lopoukhine)

1915 (Moscow)—2006 (Oxford)

my predecessor as Starosta

and from whom I learned so much

—Michael Donley

CONTENTS

A Word from the Translator

Written by one of the foremost theologians of the Russian emigration, one who had a profound influence on the Patristic renewal in contemporary Orthodox theology, this small book presents a side of the man that will be a revelation to those who know him only from his scholarly works. This in itself seemed a sufficient reason for translating the only book of Vladimir Lossky—other than his thesis on Meister Eckhart—never to have appeared in any language other than the original French.

In essence it is an extended diary, describing Lossky's departure on foot from Paris as the Germans approached the city. This was no act of cowardice, but rather an attempt to enlist in the army. As Lossky walks from one *gendarmerie* to another, being continually turned away and sent further and further south, he has time to reflect upon the meaning of suffering and on matters that have become uncannily topical again in our own day. These include the true nature of Christian or western civilisation (indeed of Christianity itself); the rightness or otherwise of war against enemy attacks on it; the problems of any relationship between Church and State; what we mean—or should mean—by 'Europe' or any 'nation'; secularisation; the problems posed by the mass movements of peoples. Here were further reasons for wishing to make the text available to an anglophone readership.

These issues are mulled over, not as arid abstractions but by someone who—as he moves across an increasingly war-torn landscape—quite literally has his feet on the ground. The text was written at one go—in a prose which is frequently poetic—at the end of the 'seven days', when the final collapse of the army had put an end to Lossky's hopes (though he did later participate in the *Résistance*). It can be argued that the experience as a whole served as a catalyst in the development of his thinking, as ideas entertained previously were brought more sharply into focus. Lossky became more than ever aware of what he perceived to be France's underlying, inner reality. He became convinced of what he perceived to be her spiritual destiny— as "a focus of regeneration for Western Christianity in a Europe that [was] already becoming de-Christianised"—and convinced of the necessary role of Orthodoxy in that destiny. It is surely no accident that several of the themes touched upon in the following pages were to be developed in his later writings; initially, not long afterwards in the lectures (given in 1944) which formed the basis of his well-known classic, *The Mystical Theology of the Eastern Church*.

Those who might imagine Vladimir Lossky to have been nothing other than a strict, even narrow-minded, defender of Eastern Orthodoxy will be surprised to discover his openness to the Christian West. Those who, misled by the rigour and precision of his academic writings, might imagine him to have been simply a dry intellectual will have the pleasure of discovering his warm humanity and fully rounded personality—further evidence of which is given in the testimonies of his children, appended to the text by the original editor, his elder son Father Nicholas Lossky.

I am grateful to Father Nicholas for his help and advice, and for reading through my translation.

Michael Donley

Preface to the original French edition of 1998

BY NICHOLAS LOSSKY[1]

The text which follows has never before been published, even though the author composed his *récit-méditation* only a few days after the events he lived through in June 1940, when the French government collapsed in chaos and people fled from Paris *en masse* as the Germans advanced ever closer. Vladimir Lossky's own peregrination across France, however, was not that of someone fleeing from invasion, as becomes obvious when one reads his account. On the contrary, he went from one *gendarmerie* to another, forever being fobbed off and directed further and further south, in an all-out attempt to enlist in the army so as to play his part in defending French soil. (He had been turned down in 1939, since he was the father of four children and, moreover, suffered from heart problems.) In the end, having failed in his venture, in his military dream, he unexpectedly met up with his family again in La Borgne, a hamlet near Martel in the *département* of the Lot, to where they had earlier been evacuated. It was there, shortly after arriving, that he wrote—at one go— *Sept jours sur les routes de France.*

[1]Vladimir Lossky's elder son (born in 1929), Nicholas Lossky is Emeritus Professor of the University of Paris-Nanterre and Professor of Western Church History at St Sergius Orthodox Theological Institute (not retired). After studying English at the Sorbonne and Theology at the Institut Saint-Denis, he then studied at St Edmund Hall, Oxford (1952–55) before submitting a doctoral thesis at the Sorbonne on Lancelot Andrewes. (This was published by Les Éditions du Cerf in 1986.) Ordained deacon of the Russian Orthodox Church in 2002 and priest in 2006, he lives in Paris and serves in the Diocese of Korsun. [Please note that the annotations in this volume are those of Michael Donley.]

The text has never been published before now because the Lossky family feared that it might be misused by certain political or religious groups. In Russia during the dark days of Soviet rule, for example, Vladimir Lossky—though recognised as a theologian by such figures as Patriarch Sergius and then by all those who took theology seriously—would have been denounced as a monarchist nostalgic for the Ancien Régime and obviously anti-revolutionary. The book would quite simply have been banned by the KGB. His other writings— translated into Russian by a friend, Vera Reschikov—made a considerable contribution to a Church reduced to silence.[2]

In France and elsewhere, people could have attempted—and still could in certain political and religious milieus—to appropriate this theologian of quality as a "man of the Right", even of the extreme Right. Likewise in post-Soviet Russia. There, ultra-conservative theologians nostalgic for the "traditional" link between Church and Nation—which they take to mean Church and State, a state headed preferably by a monarch—might wish to see in these pages support for their view that Vladimir Lossky was indeed a man after their own hearts, a "traditional" Orthodox, by which is really meant "traditionalist". They might, furthermore, feel confirmed in their nationalistic conception of Orthodoxy. Yet any such "hijacking" would be completely to misinterpret the book and indeed the person of its author. All in all, it seems essential—now that *Seven Days on the Roads of France* is being made available to a wider public—to provide a certain amount of clarification.

To begin with, it must be made clear that for this Russian Orthodox theologian—who remained very authentically Russian in many respects—France was not, as it was for many *émigrés*, simply a land of asylum. To be sure, it was that; but, above all, in his case it was a land chosen quite deliberately. Indeed his great love for the country began in childhood. It came first of all from his governess, Mlle Sophie Raylnaud, or *Maziassia* as she was called—this being the children's

---

[2]Eloquent testimony to the widespread and influential nature of this contribution is given by Metropolitan Philaret of Minsk in Issue no. 204 (Oct.–Déc. 2003) of *Contacts*, the French review of Orthodox theology and spirituality. In particular, see pages 396–7.

mispronunciation of "Mademoiselle". She became almost a member of the family, adored by the children, and never forgotten.

His love of France—and through her of the West in general—was combined very early on with a keen interest in the ideals of mediaeval chivalry. Throughout his life, Vladimir Lossky lived according to the spirit of these ideals. Indeed, his theological jousts were reminiscent of those knightly tournaments in which the fight for truth, together with complete respect for one's adversary, was allied to the most absolute intellectual honesty. It was in this spirit of knightly chivalry that he always tried to educate his children. The Confraternity of Saint Photius, of which he was for a long time the President, had for him something of the Round Table about it.[3] As for the quest for the Grail, this was understood by him as an ongoing search for the purity of Orthodoxy, wherever it might be found. These chivalrous ideas were further developed under the influence of Dimitri Vasilyevich Boldyrev, a family friend who was a specialist in the subject.

This love of France and of the Middle Ages helps us to understand why, in 1920 at the age of 17, he enrolled at the University of St Petersburg (Petrograd at the time) to follow the course of lectures given by Mme Olga Antonovna Dobiash-Rozhdestvensky on the French Middle Ages. (He studied at the University for two years, until his family was expelled in 1922.) She had lived in Paris and was a disciple of Ferdinand Lot, the eminent mediaevalist and Professor at the Sorbonne. Later, in 1924 when Vladimir Lossky himself chose to study the Western Middle Ages in Paris, he too became the pupil—and friend—of Ferdinand Lot, as well as of his wife, Myrrha Lot-Borodine, herself a Russian Orthodox theologian.[4] He also became a faithful disciple of Étienne Gilson, with whom he remained in contact until his death. (Gilson wrote the Preface for the posthumous publication, edited by

[3]Founded in 1923 and named after one of the great defenders of Orthodoxy, the Confraternity's manifesto stated that Christian unity could only be achieved by confessing Orthodoxy in its purity, something which must be reborn in the West. While remaining loyal to Moscow, the members wished to foster a genuinely Western Orthodoxy.

[4]The areas in which she specialised included the gift of tears, deification, and Nicholas Cabasilas. In 1913 she had also published another book that would have interested Vladimir Lossky: *Le Roman idyllique au Moyen Age*.

Olivier Clément, of Vladimir Lossky's doctoral thesis, *Théologie négative et connaissance de Dieu chez Maître Eckhart*.[5]

While still at the University of Petrograd, however, his studies of the Western Middle Ages acquired a new dimension under the decisive influence—one that is of incalculable significance in any attempt to understand Vladmir Lossky's destiny—of the teaching of Professor Ivan Mikhailovich Grevs. This scholar specialised in the Fathers of the Western Church, and it was he who first brought Meister Eckhart to the notice of the young student who was to devote a lifetime of research to this Rhineland mystic. This led him in turn to acquire a far-reaching and in-depth knowledge of Scholasticism, in particular of St Thomas Aquinas, whom he revered, while at the same time being critical of certain of his theological positions.

Another family friend in St Petersburg—Lev Platonovich Karsavin, who was also a Professor at the University—played an even more determining role in the orientation of the future theologian. For it was Karsavin who kindled in Vladimir Lossky an interest in the Greek Church Fathers. This was the source of his attachment to Patristic theology, of his conception of the Church and of his rootedness in her, in the spirit of the Fathers.

When, along with other eminent representatives of the intelligentsia, the family was expelled from Russia in 1922, they settled first in Prague, where a lively university activity developed. It was there that Vladimir Lossky became a student of N.P. Kondakov, the celebrated Byzantinologist who inspired more than one vocation among the Russian emigration.

In 1924 Lossky was able to make his dream come true of going to France in order to study at the Sorbonne and, at last, to discover for himself this ancient Christian land. In fact, for him, "France" was primarily a land sanctified by the blood of her martyrs and by her saints. His attachment to Saint Geneviève never ceased to deepen throughout his life. It was close to her tomb that he composed the great majority of his writings.

In order to gain a proper understanding of one of the main themes of *Seven Days on the Roads of France*, we must realize that the con-

[5]Paris, *Vrin*, 1960. Last reprinted 2002.

cept of the *nation* found in the text contains not the slightest trace of nationalism. To begin with, it is important to note that, for Vladimir Lossky, a nation's richness lies in the cultural input of the many ethnic groups that have contributed to its make-up throughout history. Secondly, his constant reference to saints shows that, in his eyes, a nation is not an abstract or ideological notion, nor a sort of unity caused by a fusion in which individuals disappear amid a certain anonymity. Rather, it is a communion of responsible persons, of which the saints represent the ideal, sanctity being the vocation of everyone. His admiration for Joan of Arc sprang not from seeing her as a symbol of an anti-English France. In her, and in Saint Geneviève, what he revered were *persons* (i.e. beings in communion) who were orientated towards God, and who discharged to the end the responsibility He conferred on them at a given moment in history, so as to struggle for peace without harbouring any hatred for the enemy. Here one can detect in outline themes that Lossky was to develop later on more than one occasion, when discussing the concept of catholicity (i.e. unity in diversity and diversity in unity, in the image of the Holy Trinity).

It is in the same light that one should understand Lossky's attachment to the idea of *monarchy*. In his eyes, the monarch's vocation is to be responsible for his people, to sacrifice himself for them to the point of giving his life, if need be, in the image of the King of kings. The true vocation of a monarch is sanctity, insofar as he is, in fact, simply the first *lay* person in the kingdom (in the word's noble sense, "member of the *laos*"). In this connection, one should read the 1954 essay entitled "Dominion and Kingship: An Eschatological Study", included as the final chapter of the book published posthumously as *In the Image and Likeness of God*.

One other term is worth defining more clearly. Several times in the following pages reference is made to *Tradition*, sometimes with a capital letter, sometimes not. Moreover, the author often evokes former times. Yet nothing would be more inaccurate than to see in this even the slightest trace of an emotional attachment to the past, of conservatism, or "traditionalism". All who knew Vladimir Lossky, and in particular all those who attended his lectures and who have followed his teachings, know what "Tradition" meant for him: nothing less than the life of the Holy Spirit in the Church. And the Spirit continues to "inspire" today just as on the day of Pentecost.

When a Christian is baptised and chrismated,[6] he receives both the fullness of Revelation and also the capacity to appropriate it so as to live it *today*, in unanimity with the "cloud of witnesses" of all ages. For there is only one Spirit. Vladimir Lossky did not accept that one could be content with repeating what others—however prestigious—had written or said. He had a holy horror of what might be called an "Orthodoxy of repetition". For him, each person is called to convert his intelligence and heart so as to become a "living stone" of the Church (1 Peter 2:5) or, as he himself put it, to acquire a "catholic conscience".

This understanding of Tradition—as something living and creative rather than passive—is clear to anyone who reads, or re-reads, the following three articles of his, articles which in fact gain from being taken together. Most important is "Tradition and Traditions", written in 1952 for the book jointly authored with Leonid Ouspensky, entitled *The Meaning of Icons*. Then there is the 1948 article "Concerning the Third Mark of the Church: Catholicity". Lastly, an article which logically follows on from this, "Catholic Consciousness: Anthropological Implications of the Dogma of the Church". (All three are included in *In the Image and Likeness of God*.)

Many other texts could be cited to illustrate the fact that for Lossky "traditional" theology—that is, theology "according to Tradition"—implies a boldness allied with the fear of God, a boldness which expresses itself in the ability to speak imaginatively of God to our contemporaries. An imagination enlightened, of course, by the Holy Spirit who "will teach you all things" (John 14:26) and "will guide you into the fullness of truth" (John 16:13).

Let me now quote the words of someone who, according to Vladimir Lossky himself, was the most gifted, the most brilliant of those who followed his teaching; namely, Olivier Clément. His long article "Vladimir Lossky, un théologien de la personne et du Saint

---

[6]In the Orthodox Church, the sacraments of Baptism and Chrismation (Confirmation) are administered on the same occasion, even for infants.

Esprit" is still probably the best study. It is based on notes that Clément took during Lossky's lectures, until the latter's death.[7]

On the notion of dogma from an Orthodox perspective, Clément writes as follows: "For Orthodoxy, Lossky insists, a dogma is not an attempt to explain a mystery or even an attempt to make it more comprehensible. Rather, it seeks to encircle the ineffable and to compel the mind to surpass itself by a clear-minded sense of wonder and adoration. [. . .] Thus a dogma is not a solution to a problem but the protection of a mystery, in the Christian sense of Revelation of the unfathomable, the inexhaustible, the *personal*. In defining a dogma, the sole aim of the Church is to preserve the possibility for each Christian of participating in Revelation with his whole being; that is, of communicating with the very life of the One who reveals Himself."

For Lossky, continues Clément, theological thought in general is "necessarily 'catholic' ", in the etymological sense of the word— "according to the whole". It is the development of truth as a whole that gives sense to each individual theme. In his opinion, whenever a difficulty arises one must, as it were, contract the fullness—by means of a veritable dogmatic 'involution'. Indeed, Lossky used to say that the composition of the rule of faith is the result of a series of conscious *involutions*, not of an organic *evolution*. Truth is a living body that cannot be dissected as if it were a corpse. [. . .] The insistence that theological thought should never deteriorate into abstract speculation was first of all—for this theologian who re-read the Bible in its entirety every year—a consequence of the *historicity* of Revelation. Biblical Revelation [. . .] is unique in being linked to the history of a people. [. . .] The Word became flesh—and the whole of Christian Revelation thereby receives a concrete, historical character."

Clément makes clear how, for Vladimir Lossky, theology is "practical" because it is "soteriological"; that is, directed towards the salvation of each and every one of us. Which is, he continues, why "theological formulations [. . .] should comprise a message for man today, should express *here and now* a witness that is forever fresh. In the fire of Pentecost, which has never been extinguished, one

[7]See "Mémorial Vladimir Lossky 1903–1958", *Messager de l'Exarchat du Patriarche russe en Europe occidentale*, No.30–31 (1959), pp. 137–206.

must ceaselessly re-express—or, better, personally recreate—the ancient dogmas. [. . .] There is no Tradition that is not living and creative, through a union between human freedom and the grace of the Holy Spirit."

Discussing Vladimir Lossky's attitude to western civilisation, Clément stresses that "he had neither the total disdain nor the blind admiration that one so often finds among Orthodox. Rather, he exhibited a positive interest, a penetrating understanding born of his increased faithfulness to Tradition. Orthodoxy gave him the freedom of love— a genuine *discernment of spirits* in the matter of culture—so that he was able to reveal as if *from within* the best aspects of western thought. One day an account must be given of just how much he loved France, and how much his instinct for Orthodoxy enabled him to uncover the deep history of French spirituality, too often hidden by Roman centralisation."[8]

Let me add a final word to Clément's assessment. The Apostles of the Last Times referred to in the message of Our Lady of La Salette— and mentioned by Vladimir Lossky more than once in the pages that follow—are all those today who seek the purity of an orthodoxy (in the non-confessional sense) that wells up from sources common to all Christians.

Nicholas Lossky

July 1997

[8]The present book, of course, itself provides such an account, in Vladimir Lossky's own words.

DAY 1

Thursday 13th June 1940

It looked like it was going to be a scorching hot day. From early morning, a sultry heat had hung over Paris, oppressive and menacing. The outskirts of the capital had an unusual look about them. Near the Porte de Versailles, groups of soldiers lay about in the shade. They looked tired and dismal—the flotsam and jetsam of a routed army. They had just come back from the front, which must have been quite near, somewhere in the Paris region. Nobody knew where, exactly. And these exhausted *poilus,*[1] who looked simultaneously sheepish yet uncomplaining, weren't saying anything. No rumbling of cannons had been heard since yesterday evening. It was a strange silence, one that got you down, intensifying the feeling of forlornness and of sheer dread in the face of the uncertain, the unknown.

Now and then military trucks drove past. Sometimes tanks that made the cobblestones vibrate, or artillery *en route* for an unknown destination. As they had done yesterday and the day before that, city dwellers were making their way towards the southern gates. On bicycles, on foot, pushing prams, carrying baggage that was in many cases too bulky and unsuitable for a long, risky journey. Were they aware of the difficulties that lay ahead? I don't know. But all of them wore a look of dreary determination, which suddenly found expression when a working-class woman cried out, "I'd rather die than become a *Boche*!"

Those who had stayed behind wandered about in the streets, looking lost, anxious, seeking in vain for a point of reference, a piece of *terra firma,* or at least some semblance of stability amidst the sudden collapse of that living structure that is any city. Some of the policemen

[1]An affectionate nickname for French infantrymen from World War One. Unusually, Lossky makes it refer to the Second World War.

were cycling off too, while those who stayed in their police stations looked just as sad and lost as the rest of the population. "We don't know anything either. You leave, if you can. We have to stay behind, to maintain order."

Order . . . It seemed to me that the State—that compact necessary to any human society, that vast fictitious reality so deeply rooted in our conscious awareness as to have become part of ourselves—it seemed that it had in fact ceased to exist. Order, on the other hand, continued to be maintained all the same, by a sort of inertia, an innate discipline, or rather by a silent solidarity between men and women who were all suffering the same fate.

As for the Third Republic—with its government, its civil servants, its law-courts, its bailiffs, its stamped documents, the entire panoply of its administrative symbols—did it still really exist? It was as if we had suddenly been transported back a thousand years to the period of the Norman invasions, to a time when the royal Carolingian line was dying out. A time when a feeling for monarchy was disappearing from people's consciousness, giving rise to other instincts. To other, more concrete, more personal bonds—trade-guilds, for example, ties between one human being and another, such as formed the basis of feudal society with its solid, male virtues.

Should one leave the city? Should one stay? Nobody knew. The authorities were either silent or contradictory in their orders, which really amounted to little more than advice. In fact, authority as such no longer existed, hadn't done so since the morning. Everyone acted according to their own conscience. Those who resigned themselves to staying in their homes, their street, their *quartier*, their city—now become a prey to enemy invasion—were right. Equally right were those whose conscience dictated that they should set out on the great adventure of the open road.

I, too, was following my conscience when I decided to leave. Three days earlier, on Monday evening, the wireless had conveyed the order issued by the Military Governor of the Seine *département*[2] addressed to all eligible men who had not yet been called up. They were to leave

[2]This included the city proper, plus 80 independent suburban communes. In 1968 it was split up into 4 smaller departments.

the Paris region within the space of six days, counting from Thursday June 13th, and to fall back to the provinces, to destinations that would be assigned them by members of the *garde mobile* stationed at the main gates leading south.

What my friend[3] and I wanted above all was to take part in the defence of Paris—for we still assumed that there would indeed be an attempt to defend the city. However, in the recruitment centre on the Rue Saint-Dominique our destiny was clarified in an unexpected manner. My friend, being a Russian refugee, tried to enlist in the Foreign Legion but was refused on account of his poor health. As for me, a French citizen, I was told that I must wait until I was called up and that I couldn't enlist beforehand. "But I want to take part in the defence of Paris," I said. The lieutenant simply shrugged his shoulders with a bitter smile. "Try to enrol in the *gardes territoriaux* at the *gendarmerie*." At the *gendarmerie* we met with the same shrugging of shoulders, the same sad smile. There was nothing for it but to "fall back to the provinces". My friend wanted to come too, but was unable to obtain in time the safe-conduct that foreigners required and in the end had to resign himself to staying put. As for me, I began to get ready to leave.

At 12.30 p.m. we heard on the wireless, the faraway muffled voice of Paul Reynaud[4] announcing that the enemy was at the city gates and that surrender was only a matter of hours away. That only a swift and immediate influx of help could save France. That there was not a moment to lose.

By 2 p.m. I was coming out of the métro at the Porte d'Orléans, along with the 18-year-old son of our neighbours.[5] Like myself, he too

[3]Maxime Kovalevsky (1903–1988), brilliant mathematician and one of the best 20th century composers of liturgical music, if not *the* best. [*Original editor's note.*]

[4]Prime Minister from March to June 1940. Like Churchill in Britain, he was almost alone in the 1930's in calling on his country to resist Nazi Germany and to prepare for armed combat. As France began to collapse in May 1940, he urged resistance and maintenance of the alliance with Britain, but Marshal Pétain and others preferred armistice with Germany. Unwilling to be a party to this, Reynaud resigned on June 16th, three days after the radio broadcast Lossky refers to, and was kept in captivity for the duration of the war.

[5]Michel Rygalov. In November 1947 he was deported, as part of retaliatory measures then being taken, and died in Moscow in 1989. [*Original editor's note.*]

was "falling back to the provinces" in order, sooner or later, to be recruited into the army. I was carrying two haversacks, one on each side, a knapsack, and a blanket slung across my shoulders. It was rather a heavy get-up, but well balanced. Besides, one needed to take along a good many provisions, without being under any illusion as to the difficulties of getting supplies once on the road.

At the Porte d'Orléans the crowd was dense. With some difficulty we eventually found a member of the *garde mobile*. He was being besieged by men waving their papers at him, all trying to enlist. I shall never forget the deep note of melancholy in the voice of this gallant constable. "You'd better leave, lads. Walk straight on to Brétigny. Report in the square there. But get going quickly. The *Boches* should have been here by now!"

The sky became overcast. A few drops of rain fell, making it easier to walk. Ahead of us stretched the road to Orléans. An ancient Roman road, one that had witnessed the passage of so many armies down the centuries. So many pilgrims, too, on their way to Santiago de Compostela, or elsewhere. So many monks, clerics, knights, and *jongleurs*—those itinerant mediaeval minstrels and entertainers. A road that passes royal abbeys and châteaux; one that has heard the hymns of Crusaders and *chansons de geste*.[6] A road trodden by countless generations of those who have made France what she is. A road of kings and saints.

Today it was crowded with a motley collection of people—sad yet determined, fierce yet profoundly human. People helped each other as they went along, without having to be asked, for everyone felt drawn closer together by a common destiny. Overloaded trucks and cars stopped every ten metres or so, blocking the way. Those with bicycles were forced to dismount in order to make any headway through the shifting mass. Groups of soldiers forced their way through. *Gendarmes*, postmen, and railwaymen had joined us, forgetting their administrative functions—which were anyway pointless now—becoming all of a sudden, despite their uniforms, unfortunate people just like the rest of us, intent on walking straight ahead. One woman was pushing a pram in which slept two babies, at times

[6]Mediaeval verse chronicles of heroic exploits.

exposed to the full heat of the sun, at times showered with rain. Ten kilometres out of Paris the two front wheels came off. The husband, who was carrying a suitcase on his shoulder, joined forces with his wife so they could keep on pushing ever further without having to stop. An elderly lady could be seen walking with difficulty and dragging along two little dogs. We quickened our pace instinctively; for we all had one thought in mind: if only we're not too late . . . We were in constant fear lest those in front should turn back, for there was a rumour that the Germans had reached Versailles . . . Fontainebleau . . . that they were everywhere, that Paris had been surrounded by their motorized columns and that we had been caught like rats in a trap. There was only one course open to us: to walk, to keep on walking.

At Longjumeau some kind people gave us fresh water to drink and filled our bottles and canteens. It was the only thing they had to offer, but what a humane gesture, what an eternally precious gift, like the "cup of cold water" in the gospels.[7] After eating a few biscuits, sitting by the roadside in the rain, we set off again and took a left fork towards Brétigny. Here the road was clearer; we could walk at a faster pace. The sun was setting, the sky calm and cloudless again. The peacefulness of the fields newly washed by rain, the smell of the wet earth and the distant cry of a cuckoo all made for a strange contrast with everything we had left behind on the highway. One or two groups of young men, some on foot, others on bikes, were making their way to Brétigny, too. We talked about what lay in store for us, expressing the hope that our journey would end successfully. That this very day we would be laying aside our civvies and putting on greatcoats and forage caps, and that perhaps tomorrow we would be setting off for a camp or a barracks somewhere in France.

We could see a plane flying over Brétigny, circling low above the rooftops—a French plane? On the town square, our papers were examined. My companion was told to remain overnight. The next morning, along with other young men, he would be put on a train for an unknown destination. As for me, being older, I was given the order to carry on to Étampes, under my own steam. Meanwhile I would

[7]Mt. 10:42.

be allowed to spend the night at a farm that had been requisitioned for refugees.

At *la ferme Chevrot* we were welcomed by a gruff but good-hearted sergeant. A place was made for us on some straw in a vast barn, alongside other men who, like ourselves, were eligible for mobilisation. The other half of the barn was sheltering families of refugees. We were each given a packet of *cigarettes de troupe*[8]—our first welcome to the army. Tomorrow I would be a real soldier. I would be allotted my own place—modest but clearly and precisely defined—among the combined operations of those whose duty it was to resist. I would have an anonymous regimental number, as one 'unknown soldier' among so many others. No longer would I be on the fringe of the common task. No longer would I be an 'intellectual', aloof from the mainstream of society—one of those sensitive, delicate beings who are constantly reconsidering things in a meditative state, and in whom normal life comes to a standstill so as to occasion thought. I would simply do my duty, without having to think, without qualms, staring with gritted teeth straight in the face of the shocking fact that was still impossible to take in: the Germans are in Paris!

Brétigny . . . The name of this the first leg of my journey preyed on my mind, causing sleep to elude me. It is a name known to every schoolboy, the name of a treaty that relinquished a third of France to the enemy.[9] Yet during the Hundred Years' War France would know more difficult moments still. The words of an old song came to mind:

> *Mes amis, que reste-t-il*
> *À ce Dauphin si gentil?*
> *Orléans, Beaugency,*
> *Notre-Dame de Cléry,*
> *Vendôme, Vendôme.*[10]

[8]Army cigarettes, not for public sale and instantly recognisable by the yellowish brown colour of their paper.

[9]The Treaty of Brétigny was signed in 1360, bringing about a 9-year period of peace in the Hundred Years' War between France and England, but ceding Gascony, Calais and Ponthieu to Edward III of England. As part of the deal, he was supposed to relinquish his claim to the French throne; but this he failed to do.

[10]The Dauphin in question was Charles VII, recognised as King by those forces

Nevertheless the enemy was, in the end, driven out of the Kingdom of France, as a consequence of the miraculous events associated with Joan of Arc, which occurred at the limit of all human hope. At the point where the human resources of valiant captains skilled in feat of arms and of wise counsellors artful in matters of politics had been exhausted. It was only then that the miracle wrought by Joan of Arc— or, rather, this heroic exploit of God—took place. When all the teaching authority of the prelates and all the theology of the Doctors had become nothing more than so much useless verbiage, powerless to revive the faith of Christian folk—empty words, similar to the foolish assertions of the "sensible" friends of Job.

Every day since the beginning of the war we too have heard idle words of counsel, words nevertheless charged with consequences. For it is always our words which convict us, which deliver us to our fate.[11]

"We shall conquer," we were told, "because we are the strongest, because we are the richest. We shall conquer because we have the will to do so."[12] As if *bons d'armements*[13] in themselves could bring about victory. As if war were nothing other than a vast industrial undertaking, a mere matter of capital. Such a war—a war of equipment and weaponry, inhuman, materialistic—yes, we have no doubt lost such a war. We must have the courage to say so. What is more, France could never have won such a war. Otherwise, she would no longer have been France, pre-eminently humane. If she *had* won such a war—one with-

---

who held the centre and south of France. However, with the support of the Bourguignons, Henry VI of England was proclaimed King of France in 1422. Charles fled to Bourges, the area he controlled being greatly reduced in size, as the above lyrics stress. It is a patriotic song, contemporary with the events themselves, that is still sung—often as a round—by scouts, for example. Its melody is also used as a carillon, known as the Carillon de Vendôme.

[11]Lossky perhaps has at the back of his mind the following verse from Matthew's Gospel (12:36): "every idle word that men shall speak, they shall give account thereof in the day of judgment".

[12]Lossky is echoing the words of Paul Reynaud, spoken in September 1939 when he was still Minister of Finance: "*Nous vaincrons parce que nous sommes les plus forts*".

[13]During the Phoney War, people had been encouraged by posters to buy these "munitions bonds".

out a human face, a war of equipment (the kind war being presented to us)—she would have lost the most precious thing she possesses, the essential characteristic of her very being. She would have lost that which makes her France, that which differentiates her from every other country on earth.

Wherever we have resisted, it has been a case of human courage, French courage, joining battle with enemy equipment superior in number and power. In spite of the laws of this 'war of equipment', people had been defending their native soil, their land. No doubt we have lost the 'war of equipment'; but war on a human scale, the French kind, this has not been lost. The Germans are in Paris;[14] perhaps they will get to the Loire, to the Garonne, everywhere. But France is not conquered yet; the 'human' war has only just begun. Perhaps it will last for a century. As during that other great period of troubles that we call the Hundred Years' War, a period which nevertheless saw the birth of a new France.

There was another heresy, too—spiritual, this time—one which sought to superimpose itself on the materialism of the 'war of equipment' argument, to infuse into it an artificial soul. This was the ideology of a 'holy war', a 'crusade'. It came in several varieties: the struggle for democracy, for freedom, for human dignity, for western culture, for Christian civilisation, even for divine justice itself. I say 'heresy' because such ideas, often just in themselves, were not based on lived experience. They did not well up from a deep, wholesome spring, which alone could have transformed them into ideas having a motivating force. Moreover, such words rang false, like all abstractions. They rang false above all since they sought to present as *absolutes*, concepts and values that are secondary, relative. For even Christian civilisation, as a civilisation, is simply a by-product, the fruition or external manifestation of a reality that *is* absolute: namely, the faith of Christian people. One does not wage a holy war on behalf of cathedrals, theological tomes or missals. These are merely the Church's vesture—Christ's vesture, that was divided among the soldiers at the foot of the Cross. As for the Church, the source of these

[14]This was true by the time Lossky came to write down his thoughts and impressions, later in June.

secondary assets, she does not need us to defend her physically, she has no need of our childish swords. It is pointless to repeat the naïve act of Peter, when he cut off the servant's ear in the Garden of Gethsemane.

No, war is not waged for absolute values. This has been the mistake of all so-called 'religious' wars, and the main cause of the atrocities associated with them. Nor is it waged for relative values that one endeavours to turn into absolutes, nor yet for abstract concepts which have been lent a religious character. Even if one were to set against the idol of a 'pure race' the more benign idols of Law, Liberty and Humanity, they are still idols—concepts that have been personified and made into absolutes.[15] This would still result in a war of idols. The only just war—in so far as a war may ever be styled just—is a war for relative values, for values known to be relative. A war in which man—a being destined for an absolute end—sacrifices himself spontaneously and without hesitation for a relative value that he knows to be relative: his native soil, his land, his country. It is the very sacrifice that acquires a value that is absolute, incorruptible, eternal.

The purpose of Joan of Arc's divine mission, for example, was itself relative: to lead the Dauphin to Rheims in order to give France back her king. She felt no animosity towards the English soldiers whom it was her duty to drive out of France. This is one of the main features of the 'human' warfare that she waged. It is also a distinctive characteristic of the soul of France herself, of whom Joan is the most perfect image.

In Paris there had also been talk of Justice, even of divine justice, in the name of which we ought to fight, so that this justice—understood as one of God's attributes—might triumph over the iniquity of our adversaries. "Our cause is just, which is why God will grant us victory." So spoke the prelates, the spiritual leaders of the people. It is true that just causes often did triumph in *les jugements de Dieu*, those mediaeval judicial duels fought by two parties in litigation. But in these both sides *renounced* all claims as to the justice of their cause,

[15]One is inevitably reminded of the name—*L'Humanité*—of France's communist newspaper, a journal whose status (ironically, in the light of Lossky's criticisms) was at its highest in the decade immediately following the war.

so as to give the opportunity for divine justice alone to reveal itself, without appeal, in their feat of arms. Even so, the Church was compelled to oppose this practice, 800 years ago.[16]

I had heard a distinguished prelate speak about the justness of our cause in Notre Dame before thousands of the faithful, beseeching God to grant us victory in the name of this just cause. Were one to pursue his line of thought, one would have to conclude that God was obliged to help us—since He is just, and we were defending justice. He could not act or wish otherwise without contradicting Himself, without renouncing His attribute of Justice—unchangeable, as is everything that is written about Him in the compendiums and manuals of theology. If, then, we were in the end to lose this war, after having implored God to grant us victory in the name of His justice, what would remain to be said? One of two things: either our cause was not, in fact, just; or else God Himself is unjust.

Yes, if you like, He is unjust, in the sense that He is greater than Justice, because His justice is not our justice, nor His ways our ways.[17] Because, compared to His justice, which will one day cause the foundations of the universe to founder, our own poor justice amounts to nothing more than injustice.

Prayers for victory ought to have been accompanied by tears and profound contrition, mindful of this awesome Justice, before which we are always unjust. Any appeal ought to have been made, not to God's justice—which is not commensurate with ours, and which we could not withstand—but to His infinite mercy, which caused His Son to come down from Heaven.

> *"Lord, we are always unjust in Thy sight, and our justice is of no account; but because we are unjust and blind, not knowing how to fathom Thy ways, come to our aid. Withold Thy sword of justice and grant us victory over the enemy whom Thou hast*

---

[16]A reference to the mediaeval method of determining guilt or innocence termed *justicium Dei*. These trials by combat (known in England as 'wagers of battle') were based on the idea that God would help the innocent party by guaranteeing his victory. The practice—pagan in origin—was condemned by the 4th Lateran Council in 1215.

[17]See Isaiah 55:8.

permitted to invade France. For nothing comes about except it be Thy will, and Thou art the Master of all the peoples of the earth, whom Thou chastiseth for their greater good."

But the blindness of secular, 'self-determined' morality had been hardening hearts, even those of churchmen. People had long since forgotten what was known by Philippe de Commines, discerning political historian and wise counseller of Louis XI: "Thus it is true that God is almost forced or summoned to show many signs and to punish us in many ways on account of our stupidity or, which is more likely, our wickedness. [. . .] Who but God can remedy things?"[18]

Less than three weeks ago, on Sunday May 26th, a vast crowd had filled the Place du Panthéon and the streets neighbouring the church of Saint-Étienne-du-Mont.[19] The reliquary of Saint Geneviève was carried about in procession, followed by bishops and canons. It was the first time in decades that the saint had left her sanctuary. For, after all, people wanted to have recourse to her protection. The protection of the one who had halted the indomitable onslaught of the Huns, who had saved the city, altering—perhaps by her prayers—the destiny of France, which was to be decided on the plain of Catalaunum.[20]

Everyone in the crowd knew, we all knew, that a great battle was taking place in Flanders, that several of our close relatives were in mortal danger, and had perhaps already been killed. We knew that France herself was in danger. Yet the sky was blue and the summer sun

[18]Philippe de Commines (1447–c.1511) has been described as "the first critical and philosophical historian since classical times" (*Oxford Companion to English Literature*). Lossky's quote comes from Book 5, Ch. 18 of his *Mémoires*, begun in 1488. Yet so steeped is de Commines' thought in the necessity for statesmen of trusting in God that Lossky could have quoted from almost any chapter.

[19]Where St Geneviève's shrine is to be found.

[20]The Battle of the Catalaunum Fields in 451 (thought to have taken place near Châlons-en-Champagne) is considered by many historians to have been one of the most important battles of Late Antiquity, for the fate of western civilization hung in the balance. It had the effect of halting the advance of the Huns, led by Attila. Earlier, during his advance on Paris, Geneviève (c.420–c.500) repeatedly advised people to stay in their homes and not abandon their city, even though her words occasioned opposition and malicious criticism. Attila's turning off to Orléans was attributed to her prayers.

shone out of that Parisian sky that is without equal in the world. People prayed. The high-pitched chanting of women and children rose up from the crowd. But a certain levity gained hold of peoples' hearts, a lack of concern that they were only too willing to take for hope. The saint will protect her city, her country. We don't need to worry, nothing needs to change. The result was that this service of supplication seemed more like a fête, after which everyone went home light-hearted and carefree. My two sons played with other children, sailing a toy yacht in the Jardin du Luxembourg. We had put our trust in Saint Geneviève, patron of Paris, our patron, and we remained calm and smiling. But the saints walk in God's ways, which are not our ways . . .

The very next day, the surrender of the King of Belgium opened to the Germans the road to Paris.

Friday 14th June

A t 4 a.m., just before dawn, I bid farewell to my travelling companion and set off for Étampes. At this early hour, the road was practically deserted. Without hurrying, I walked behind several army waggons that were being pulled along by mules. The convoy was headed by Senegalese soldiers on horseback, silent and haughty.

At Arpajon, we rejoined the congested highway with its throng of refugees. At every step, scenes of misery and woe were being repeated. Always the same. Wailing on all sides, tales of distress not unlike those heard by Dante on the precipitous roads of the circles of Hell. A woman with two children looked in vain for her husband, whom she had lost from sight in the crowd yesterday. Not knowing whether to go on or whether to stop and wait, she cried in despair. Another woman had left home in such haste that, although she had dragged along four of her children, she had forgotten about the fifth, the smallest, which was still in its cot in Paris. The vehicle in which she was travelling could not stop or go back for the baby. And all the time, alarming rumours were spreading: the Germans are not far away, they are following us. We must hurry to Étampes, where we will surely find a train.

At the crossroads in Arpajon, a sergeant—a Moroccan who sported a blissful smile—was playing the policeman. To all who had the misfortune to have recourse to his superior knowledge, he indicated the same direction, with a triumphant gesture. As a result, troops, military convoys and families of refugees all went off towards La Ferté-Allais, instead of taking the correct turning to Étampes, which was a little further on. I was one of those credulous enough to trust his advice, which cost me a detour of several kilometres.

Eventually, by taking footpaths across the fields, I got back onto the correct road and set off again for Étampes, ultimate goal of my long, complicated journey. A safe haven where I would finally cease being a "private individual" and become a member of the collective body of those engaged in the noble task of defending France.

The Beauce agricultural plain stretched out on either side of the road as far as the eye could see, flat and monotonous. One road led off to the right in the direction of Chartres. Involuntarily, I was reminded of Péguy and his pilgrimage on foot along these very roads, making for Notre-Dame de Chartres to whom he was bringing the compliments of Notre-Dame de Paris. As long as the France of Péguy exists—simple and upright, with that human, peasant uprightness that is the uprightness of shepherds as well as of the kings of Chartres cathedral[1]—as long as this France exists, we have nothing to fear from any enemy invasion. For this France is eternal, older perhaps than Rome, the so-called Eternal City.[2]

[1]Just below the religious figures on the west façade are statues of kings (and queens). When sculpted in the 12th century, they were regarded as images of current monarchs. The placing of royalty lower than Christ, but still close to Him, symbolised the relationship believed to exist between the monarchs and God, with the implication that they had been ordained and put in place by Him.

[2]It is not difficult to see why Lossky was an admirer of Charles Péguy (1873–1914). To begin with, he wrote several long poems in praise of Geneviève and Joan of Arc, as well as two plays devoted to the latter. Again, like Lossky he was keen to fight in defence of France. It is said that when World War I was declared, he left off writing in mid-sentence in order to sign up. Sadly, he was killed on the first day of the First Battle of the Marne. Like Lossky, although Péguy believed in personal sacrifice, he too was adamant that this should be on behalf of concrete realities such as "hearth and home", rather than abstractions.

In *Notre Patrie* (1905), Péguy had praised the traditions of Old France, stressing that she was the land of liberty, a true heir to Graeco-Latin civilisation, and a Christian nation *par excellence*. He was passionately concerned with what he called her "eternal salvation", rather than merely her political survival. Understandably, his popularity and fame increased at the time of the Second World War.

Lossky would also have warmed to Péguy's denunciation of the spiritual aridity of modern rationalism and its obsession with abstractions. Péguy's own thought was characterised by an overriding belief that the carnal and the temporal are, despite everything, permeated by the spiritual and the eternal. In fact, one of his favourite terms was "la mystique", mystical theology—though it is important not to construe

The magical name of Étampes was on everyone's lips. We were walking there as if to some Promised Land. If only we get there in time, if only we manage to catch a train. Along with others, I climbed onto a vehicle that had stopped in the middle of the road. But no sooner had it set off than, two kilometres further on, it stopped again, at a complete standstill, having run out of petrol. I had seen hundreds like it along the highway, immobile, stuck indefinitely where they were. And so many others in the ditches, by the roadside, broken down, mere carcasses of machines . . . It was back to walking on foot.

The sun was high in the sky and it was beginning to get hot. I selected a shady spot to have some lunch and a rest. It was the grounds of an old château long since abandoned, untended and wild. The grass was tall and uncut, and had spread onto the path. Ivy had climbed up the pedestals of the statues, winding round the delicate bodies of the stone nymphs. Over the tall entrance gate, a count's coronet could still be seen. Of the château itself, however, nothing remained except part of the Louis XV façade. The wild thyme smelt good. I stretched myself out on the soft grass for a while and forgot about the highway that, a stone's throw away, was carrying thousands of people to a new destiny.

I think it was about noon by the time I finally reached Étampes. The congestion here was at its height. Cars could scarcely make any headway at all and came to a halt every few metres. Everywhere could be heard whistles, cries, the throbbing of car engines. The crowd went

---

the adjective in its popular sense. Inevitably, this brings to mind the title of Lossky's own *magnum opus*—*The Mystical Theology of the Eastern Church*—written only a couple of years after the events described in this seven-day diary.

Péguy's walked to Chartres more than once on a pilgrimage of intercession. Lossky's wording (in the sentence referring to Notre Dame) probably derives from the fact that in the long poem *La Tapisserie de Notre Dame*, one section had been styled "Présentation de Paris à Notre Dame". In this, the poet dedicated the city to the Mother of God. A later section is entitled "Présentation de la Beauce à Notre Dame de Chartres". It contains evocative descriptions of the vast sea of cornfields from within which rise the spires of the cathedral. It is just such a scene which illustrates the cover of the French original of the present book. In his own wanderings along the roads of France, did Lossky have at the back of his mind such lines from this poem as the following: "la route nationale est notre porte étroite"?

beserk, as people rushed to the railway station. As for me, I carried on making my way to the *gendarmerie*, the goal of my aspirations. Just then someone called out to me. I turned round smartly and saw a woman standing by a truck. It was a Parisian neighbour from the same floor, someone unknown and yet at the same time familiar, one of those people you greet mechanically on the stairs without knowing their name. We both gave vent to an expression of joyful surprise, as if we were old friends or close relatives who had just met up again.

She suggested I climb aboard, as there was still room for one more. They were going to Orléans, and perhaps further still. I resolutely refused, stating that I had all but reached the goal of my journey. She looked at me as if I had taken leave of my senses. "Do you really think you'll be able to find a *gendarmerie*! Anyway, the war's going to be over soon! They're supposed to be signing the armistice this evening. There isn't an army anymore! You don't have to report anywhere! He's mad, this man! Come back, Monsieur! . . . I'll keep the place for you, all the same."

I carried on walking down Étampe's cluttered main road, skirting the long line of trucks with their deafening engines. Suddenly there was an ominous noise that drowned out all the other machine-made sounds. I looked up. Three grey planes—bombers, bulky and threatening—were flying low, straight towards us. I had no time to think or move. A bomb exploded quite nearby, to my right, somewhere near the railway station. I could see wood and iron debris being thrown into the air. A second bomb blew up a tanker two hundred metres ahead. I could hear the popping noise of machine-gun fire. I threw myself to the ground, at the foot of a wall. All of this lasted for less than a second. The smell of gunpowder was everywhere. The stout man lying next to me mistook it for gas and believed he was about to die. I had great difficulty in reassuring him. Everything that had just been happening had been so unexpected, so abrupt and swift that, in my case, any reaction such as fear or panic was impossible, since nothing lasted long enough to take shape or sink into one's consciousness. I had the strange impression of witnessing a child's game: fireworks going off, cardboard buildings set on fire, the harmless rat-a-tat of toy machine-guns echoing high overhead.

After a few minutes, I got up and started off again. I went up to a policeman and asked the way to the *gendarmerie*. He grabbed me by the shoulder, shouting, "Take cover! They're coming back!" The planes did indeed come back, machine-gunning the convoy again. I just had time to dive into a nearby courtyard and take shelter in a cellar. A woman was howling, while a workman uttered cries of rage against "this government of traitors" and demanded an armistice.

Before long we could hear that the bombers were moving away, pursued by our fighter planes. I emerged from my shelter. The tanker was still in flames. In the town centre, several houses were still on fire. Here and there, black smoke rose into the air. An old man staggered along, blood streaming from his temple. Further on, a shapeless object was being loaded into a car. Out of the window poked the heads of two fair-haired children, who were lying alongside the body of their mother. I could vaguely make out some gruesome, bloody rags.

In order to avoid the fires, I had to take an adjoining street. There I passed a member of the Civil Defence who was pushing a wheelbarrow. In it lay a delirious woman with wide open, staring eyes. The smoke from the fires now rose all the way up to the old, ruined castle keep, which still dominated its town, though unable to protect it, as it once had, from brazen enemy raids.

Near the town hall, in front of the office entrance on the main square, a lieutenant was stationed, along with two sergeants and a few soldiers. With a heavy heart, I spoke to him, not expecting a positive reply. I wasn't mistaken. "Get out of here quickly! The Major is seeing nobody! Any men from Paris eligible for mobilisation are to make their way to Orléans under their own steam."

I made my way to the *gendarmerie* nevertheless, for one last attempt. A group of *gendarmes* standing around under the entrance porch, machine-guns in hand, were on the lookout for a new arrival of bombers. Their response was the same. "But," I asked, "at least give me some document or other to prove that I did report here". Obviously I was not yet freed from the bureaucratic habits of the Third Republic. The *gendarme* who replied this time was less backward than myself in this respect, more independent. "It's no longer a matter of papers or certificates. This isn't the time for red tape. That's what's been our downfall! Right now, everyone must fend for himself. Go to Orléans!"

In spite of everything, I felt reassured. For, actually, here was a case of the spirit of initiative gaining the upper hand over an ingrained enslavement to routine administrative habits and the magic formulae of officialdom. Ever since the Roman conquest, I believe, French institutions have exhibited this double strand: the *esprit gaulois*, characterised by initiative; and the *esprit latin*, one of conventional bureaucratic formalities. The former has brought with it the vitality and power that derive from the land—when it hasn't resulted in revolutionary anarchy. The latter has ensured the functioning of a civil service both wise and stupid, even if logical. For order and absurdity, logic and stupidity, can very well co-exist in government officials, that special breed of men. Down the ages, it has sometimes been Gallic initiative, sometime Latin bureaucracy that has prevailed, counterbalanced by that sense of moderation that France shares with ancient Greece, a country which—before Rome—was Gaul's tutor.[3] No, the *esprit latin* is not the *esprit français*. It is merely one component of something that in the end resists analysis: the spirit of a nation. The *esprit latin* is but one element among the many others which have gone into the making of the France we know. Like all the talents acquired during the course of her history, this mind-set of the "Latin" civil servant has at times favoured the nation's development. But at others—having assumed monstrous proportions—it has held it back, even to the extent of putting the country in mortal danger. All in all, for now, one had to free oneself from Latin bureaucracy and, as things stood, find other means of managing.

Leaving behind the horrors of Étampes, I set off down the main road in the direction of Orléans. After 5 kilometres or so, I had to stop. My swollen feet refused to take me any further. The old body, usually so biddable, was beginning to break down. I thought of the many crippled cars abandoned by the roadside. I needed to take my

---

[3]Marseilles—France's oldest city—was founded in 600 B.C. by Ionian settlers from near Ephesus. Greek culture and language spread along the coast and the immediate hinterland. Marseilles itself remained a centre of Greek learning long after the Roman invasion.

shoes off and take care of my feet. Oh, if only by a second stroke of luck I could find again the hospitable truck in which my neighbour had been travelling! Just then two Moroccan soldiers ran past me, stooping low. They signalled that I should follow them. Barefoot, I ran after them and sought shelter in a ditch under some bushes. German planes had just been attacking an airfield close by. Once again, the crackle of machine-gun fire could be heard overhead. But it didn't last long.

We had to walk briskly so as to get over this dangerous terrain as quickly as possible. In fact, there were two airfields, one on either side of the road, a few kilometres apart. I limped along, gritting my teeth and wincing in pain. When we got to Mondésir, sentries positioned near the airfield strongly urged us to continue on our way without delay. So we kept on walking, exhausted though we were. A kilometre further on, I lay down on the grass. It was impossible to take another step. The prospect of a bomb or a machine-gun bullet, far from frightening me, seemed sweet, a release, a way out. I don't how long I lay there by the roadside, half dazed. But in the end the life-force within me triumphed. With a supreme effort of will, I stood up and set off walking again.

I dragged myself along in this state as far as Monnerville. As it was still daylight, it would have been possible to travel even further and I hadn't accomplished my projected day's itinerary. It couldn't be helped, I would have to stop here. I went into a large farmyard, where a reception centre had been set up in the barns. The straw was dirty, as were the people who slept beside me. But a fraternity of misery, of the sort born at the lowest point of common degradation, brought us together. We forgot everything, save the very human feeling of solidarity in misfortune. It was on the roads of France that I got to know this feeling. Never shall I forget it.

We didn't have a calm night. Several times we heard the drone of a German plane, with its irregular engine noise—booming and melancholy, in the "romantic" style.[4] A few bombs exploded in the distance, perhaps at Mondésir. "There go the *Boches* again, gallivanting

---

[4]The allusion is musical. In the France of Couperin, Debussy and Ravel, the Wagnerian style has not always been popular.

somewhere or other," muttered a woman as she dozed. Woken by the noise, pigeons fluttered about in the rafters.

Saturday June 15th

At daybreak, I found that I could still walk after all, though I had to limp a little. I decided I would make use of any charitable offers of lifts, as this would be the only way I could reach Orléans—still more than 50 kilometres away—by the end of the day. The sun had not yet risen when I left the farm at Monnerville.

I was obliged to stop several times to give my feet a rest. Sitting by a haystack well away from the road, I listened to the conversation of two well-equipped Belgians in whose company I had been walking. One of them noted that there were far fewer people on the road today. The other replied in a sad, solemn tone of voice, "What do you expect? It's the survival of the fittest." "But," continued the first, "remember that poor old woman yesterday? The one who collapsed on the road . . . I can't get her out of my mind." "Shut up!" replied his companion. "There's no point . . . ."

A few steps further on, I came across a family sitting round a fire. They asked eagerly for any news. "Have the Germans reached Paris? We don't know anything. We've been on the road for four days. Our truck broke down . . . We're staying in the fields."[1]

As for offers of lifts, they weren't easy to come by. Finally, however, a truck did stop, a few kilometres the other side of Angerville. An elderly workman offered me a hand. I climbed aboard with my various bags and settled down, high up on top of some sacks. As the truck sped along, I experienced a feeling of intense pleasure on seeing the milestones pass by in quick succession.

We stopped at Artenay to give a lift to an elderly woman who was carrying a baby. Its mother had stayed behind in Paris, she explained.

[1] The Germans had, in fact, entered Paris the previous day.

She herself had been the charwoman and had brought the baby with her. She wanted to adopt it and intended to carry on working so as to be able to raise the child. "What do you expect?" she exclaimed. "We've got to behave like human beings. We're not animals!"

A middle-class family travelling with us—two women, two girls and a boy—were having a discussion which I listened to with great pleasure. They were saying that those who still wanted to resist the enemy should fall back as far as the Pyrenees, if necessary, but should stand fast—ready to fight along the Loire, the Garonne, or the Adour. These were the very words of Henri de Kérillis that I had read two weeks earlier in Paris.[2]

Yet what if we ran out of the space necessary to continue this great struggle? For the first time, I was seized by a feeling of doubt; for the territory of France is a limited, finite entity. Was there, I wondered, an alternative base of operations, some other terrain, stable and permanent, one that no enemy invader could penetrate. Is it not written, "Be not afraid of them which kill the body, but are not able to kill the soul; but rather fear him which is able to destroy both soul and body in hell"?[3] Thus, the only realm totally free from enemy invasion, our only true *lebensraum*,[4] infinite in riches and strength, is to be found in God. Were it to be projected onto another level, our combat would have access to new, unlimited resources, forgotten for centuries but ever-present in our spiritual subsoil. It would no longer be a "war of equipment"—that we have lost, anyway. It would no longer even be a "human" war that we have not lost yet but that we may well lose. For, however much man may want to be a hero, he remains nonetheless a being of limited capabilities. Rather, it will become an interior struggle in which God will fight with us against ourselves, a purifying and salutary struggle.

[2]Henri de Kérillis was a journalist, a newspaper editor, and an M.P. He had voted against the Munich Agreement, having denounced Hitler as early as 1936.

[3]Mt. 10:28.

[4]Given the context, Lossky's original '*espace vital*' is best translated by this German term, which he undoubtedly had at the back of his mind and which was such an important component of Nazi ideology, motivating its expansionist policy. It figures prominently, of course, in *Mein Kampf*, which Lossky will mention by name a few lines later.

What other combat could prevail against such a one as this? Hitler's *Mein Kampf* will always be so much childish prattle when set against the eternal battle of the gospels. *Nubiculum est, transibit.* It is but a little cloud, it will pass. So said one of the early Church Fathers.[5]

How many clouds have already passed? Wasn't the Frankish conquest itself a Germanic invasion? But Saint Geneviève, who repelled the Huns, was quite happy for Gaul to be seized by these Franks. For the saints walk in God's way which are not our ways, but in which we ought nevertheless to walk, if we would triumph with them. The centuries which saw the first French kings, the Merovingians, and which seem so obscure to us, lost in the mists of time when seen through the accounts of Gregory of Tours and Frédégaire,[6] were in fact a period of intense spiritual combat, waged by saints for the soul of France. The spiritual sphere—namely, grace—enveloped and penetrated the country's temporal, earthly dimension, transforming it from within.[7] St Remi, for example, made Clovis descend into the baptismal waters, as meek as a lamb.[8] Other saints, wild and superhuman like the prophets of Israel, made cruel, rapacious kings tremble with fear. A

[5]The reference seems to be to the reputed reply of St Athanasius to friends who lamented his banishment by Emperor Julian the Apostate in the 4th C.

[6]Gregory's *History of the Franks* is well known; less so the *Chronicle of Fredegar*, which covers the years 584 to 641. Successive editors continued the chronicle up to 768, the year of Charlemagne's coronation.

[7]Lossky's French here contrasts the *spirituel* and the *charnel* in a way which seems to be a further echo of Péguy. Certainly, they were two of the latter's own favourite words. Indeed, the theme which dominated his writings was a strongly Incarnational belief in the '*ligature*' (the binding together) of the spiritual and the eternal with the material, the temporal, the everyday. He even coined the phrase '*le surnaturel naturel*', to express a view which chimes with Orthodox theology more than with Western Christianity's traditional understanding of nature and grace.

[8]Saint Remi (Remigius) was remarkably gentle, meek and retiring, yet he exuded an air of majesty as well as serenity. He became Archbishop of Rheims at the age of 22. It was in the cathedral there—on Christmas Day in 496—that Clovis (fifth Merovingian king), who loved Remi, was baptised along with his army, becoming France's first Christian king. Remi died at an advanced age in 533, leaving his famous *Testament*, in which he predicted God's grace on this blessed kingdom, as long as its rulers remained faithful to Him.

new France was being born, one which later—in the *Chanson de Roland*—would be called "France la sainte".[9]

However, will we know how to rediscover this secret deposit, this treasure of uncreated powers? Or will it remain forever buried in our historical soil, covered over by other layers which—superimposed in the course of centuries—have hidden it from our eyes, becoming in their turn the new spiritual patrimony of France? Is French Christianity capable of undergoing spiritual renewal? Of bringing about a total transfiguration which would cause to gush forth again springs of living water from the parched earth of its Church? These springs have not dried up, but flow deep underground appearing only to the eyes of the simple, the humble. It was the ordinary Christian folk of France who recognised that Joan of Arc's mission was divine, something denied by the prelates and the doctors of the Sorbonne. It was to Bernadette that Our Lady of Lourdes appeared, causing a stream of consolation and regeneration to flow. It was to two children at La Salette that the Beautiful Lady—she who wept[10]—announced the anger of her Son which hung over the West, predicting the crisis of Christian faith but also the mission of the "Apostles of the Last

---

[9]*La Chanson de Roland*—the oldest major work of French literature—is also the oldest and finest *chanson de geste*. The earliest known manuscript dates from the mid-12th C, though it is loosely based on events that took place in the 8th C, during the reign of Charlemagne. Lossky's reference is to verse 2311 of this epic poem; in particular, the phrase which in the original reads "*France l'asolue*". Scott Moncrief renders this incorrectly as "France the Free". Preferable is Dorothy Sayers' version, which has 'blest France'. This is closer to the verb *asoldre*, i.e. literally, 'to absolve' (*absoudre* in modern French). However, Lossky's adjective—the one commonly found in translations into modern French—most accurately conveys the meaning.

[10]Crying she was, when the children first saw her. Yet Lossky's phrase inevitably brings to mind the title of Léon Bloy's celebrated 1908 book on the subject and which Lossky had undoubtedly read: *Celle qui pleure*. Significantly, the 19th of September—the date of the Virgin's appearance—comes shortly after the feast-day (15th) of Our Lady of Sorrows. Another reason why Lossky was fond of La Salette must surely be—as Fr Nicholas Lossky agrees—its similarity to the Orthodox feast of Pokrov, or the Protecting Veil of the Mother of God (October 1), so beloved by Russians. In that apparition too (at Constantinople), the Virgin was seen to be weeping.

Times" through whom the Holy Spirit would re-establish the Church, renewed amid suffering.

Lourdes is now dominated by an awful basilica. A mawkish and sickly sweet piety has all but smothered the miracle, the religious fact itself, so sober and pure. An abstract, legalistic dogma—namely, the privilege granted to the Virgin in view of the "future merits" of her Son—has distorted the meaning of the simple words spoken by the Mother of God to a shepherdess on the feast day of the Annunciation: "I am the Immaculate Conception".[11]

[11]Lossky was later to expand on the view sketched out here, pointing out that the words were not spoken on December 8th (the feast of Mary's own conception) but on March 25th (the Annunciation) and referred to the conception by her of Christ. See, for example, his article on the Immaculate Conception in *Messager de l'Exarchat du Patriarche russe*, déc. 1954. This was actually written in 1942, thus not long after the present *Journal*. He returned to the topic in *The Mystical Theology*, p.140f. In support of Lossky's interpretation is the fact that, at her parish priest's insistence, Bernadette had already asked the Lady for her name three times and got no reply. Why did the Lady wait until the feast of the Annunciation before answering?

Of interest from an Orthodox point of view is the incident reported (in his own words) by Fabisch, the sculptor of the official statue in the grotto. He tells us that, when he showed Bernadette a portfolio containing previous celebrated depictions of the Virgin, she hardly paid any attention. "Then, all of a sudden," he writes, "as we passed an engraving or lithograph of the Virgin of Saint Luke, she quickly put out her hand and said: 'There is something there'." She then added, "But that's not it! No, that's not it!" (See Vol. 3 of *Lourdes, histoire authentique des apparitions* by René Laurentin, p.214.) The reference is to an icon in the Byzantine style, known as Notre Dame de Grâce de Cambrai, after the town in whose cathedral it is now situated. Probably painted in Sienna c.1340, it is an Italianate copy of what is now termed the Vladimir Mother of God, probably the most beautiful of all icons. Traditionally, it is indeed said to have been "written" by St. Luke.

In the end, Bernadette's advice as to precisely how the Virgin looked was sought only to be ignored. Inevitably, she was greatly dissatisfied with the statue that was eventually installed in the grotto. Her misgivings concerned the way Lourdes was developing in general. Yet it is only fair to add that all of the vulgarity and commercialisation put together have been unable to detract from the ongoing miracle evidenced in this town. For it is a place where the world is turned upside down, where the sick, the handicapped and the dying are no longer pushed to the margins of society but day after day take their place centre stage.

As for the revelations of Notre Dame de La Salette, it took the courage of a Pope Leo XIII to publish them in the face of the protests of the majority of the clergy.[12] Yet how many people today have read the original text? It has become lost amid a diffuse tide of sentimental and anaemic literature—styled "devotional"—that has nothing in common with true religion, which by its very nature is foreign to all that is false.

Yet, will we know how to purify these springs, how to clear the way for new springs, how to work with the Apostles of the Last Times?

By now we were approaching Orléans. At last, I thought, a calm town immune as yet from the fever of evacuation. Here, at last, my destiny would be determined. However, I was immediately obliged to change my opinion. Columns of black smoke were rising on the horizon: Orléans had just been bombed. Our convoy progressed slowly forward, being forced to stop several times. At a bend in the road, we saw a male corpse lying face down in a ravine. One more victim of the law of the survival of the fittest . . .

I got down from the truck near the Park, not far from the railway station, and made my way as usual to the *gendarmerie*. Suddenly my attention was seized by a certain street name: Saint Aignan. I turned on my heels and headed straight for the cathedral, quite ashamed of myself. I had forgotten that Orléans was the seat of this great bishop. That, just like St Geneviève in Paris, he had halted the Huns at the very

[12]La Salette—a small settlement some 50 km south of Grenoble—is the site of an apparition of the Virgin Mary that took place in 1846, i.e. well before Lourdes (1858) but just 18 months before publication of the Communist Manifesto. Two children—Mélanie (15) and Maximin (11)—were looking after a few cows in a high alpine pasture when they saw a 'beautiful lady' who was weeping—because of the world's increasing sinfulness, it transpired. She charged them with a sober, but eminently biblical, message—essentially a call for people to take their faith more seriously. In this post-Revolutionary period, considerable laxity had set in.

The site of the apparition, in its impressive alpine setting, is less commercialised than Lourdes and was a favourite place of pilgrimage for Lossky. One of his last acts before dying was to accept from his daughter Marie a sip of holy water from La Salette. See her account on p. 93.

ramparts of the city.[13] Before doing anything else, I felt I had to venerate his relics, for it was he who was the real master of the place. But where were they to be found? Nobody could tell me, and my question probably seemed ridiculous. The terrified population was busy packing its bags. The town was being evacuated.

The recent explosions had shattered the windows of the department stores. Several houses were still in flames. I made my way through the débris. Refugees were sitting about on the pavement, disheartened, having no strength left to continue their journey. In front of the cathedral, by the equestrian statue of Joan of Arc, a few soldiers were harnassing draught-horses to some waggons. The horses were whinnying and striking the paving-stones with the iron of their shoes.

Alone, I went into the cathedral, with its bright, lofty vaulted ceiling and its relative absence of stained glass windows. The usual gloom shot through with the shimmering of a thousand colours that one normally encounters in such places was replaced by the unexpected clear light of day. My footsteps echoed in the empty building.

Suddenly I was struck by the sound of a hoarse, muffled voice. I was not alone, after all. A tall old man with a stoop, wearing an old-fashioned fin-de-siècle frock coat, was waving his arms about, threatening and cursing someone. He had a fine face, the look of a well-bred provincial gentleman, a devout and God-fearing type. I drew nearer, to see who he was so angry with. He was going round the cathedral, stopping before each statue of a saint. It was to them that he was addressing his curses, his cries, his threats. "*Alors, quoi?* Damn it all, then! Don't you want to help us? Can't you help us?"

I left the cathedral, quite overcome. You really needed to have a faith that was deep and sincere, a genuine inner freedom before God and His saints, to be able to talk to them like that. No, he wasn't a madman. Rather, a noble Christian soul, seized with despair and bitterness, pouring out his pain to the saints, who remained motionless and silent, guides of the divine ways that are so painful for us to follow.

At Orléans—as at Brétigny, as at Étampes—the authorities in the *gendarmerie* directed me yet further south. "Make your own way to

---

[13]St Aignan (Anianus), 358–453, was the Bishop whose prayers, it is believed, caused Attila to abandon his intention of attacking the town in 451.

Vierzon and Bourges. We're in the middle of an evacuation, here!" I went to the railway station. No more trains. It was a question of taking to the road again. Before setting off, I sat down on some grass amid dusty flowers in a public square. In committing this misdemeanour, this infringement of municipal laws and customs, I was only following the example of other refugees. While eating my lunch, I got chatting to an unfortunate woman from Brittany who was trying to get to Rennes. Her state of panic was made worse by her complete ignorance of geography. She assured me, for example, that the Germans were already at Laval and that they were expected to reach Orléans by that evening.[14]

On the main bridge, I turned round for one last look at the town that had once been saved by Joan of Arc. The cathedral, its belfry, and the old rooftops were bathed in sunlight. The Loire, sandy and slow-moving, flowed—or, rather, stagnated—under the bridge. It is an ancient stone bridge, one that now trembled under the weight of military convoys, cannons, cars of all descriptions, troops and refugees hurrying on their way, shoulder to shoulder, making headway with difficulty. A few hours later, like all the other the bridges over the Loire, it would be blown up.

Three kilometres further on, at Olivet, we crossed the Loiret and found ourselves in open countryside once more. On either side of the road were swampy meadows and occasional ponds. A typical Sologne landscape. Next to the road, on the right, was an expanse of undergrowth. Further in the distance, on the left bank of the river, a forest could be seen—vestige of those great forests abounding in game that once surrounded Orléans.

We were in the very centre of France, where the ancient provinces of the Île-de-France, Aquitaine and Burgundy meet. The mysterious centre of Gaul where the *ombilic,* the sanctuary of the Druids, was thought to be located.[15] Sacred assemblies gathered here each year, legislative councils of the ancient Celts that ensured the religious unity

[14]Laval is far to the west of Orléans, close to Rennes. The Germans advance was, of course, from the north-east.

[15]For the ancient Druids, the Forest of Orléans was indeed considered to be the *ombilic*, or *omphalos*, the symbolic centre of Gaul.

of the independent tribes of Gaul, long before the Romans imposed on them a unity of a merely political sort.

As for councils, Gaul has always recognised their supreme authority. France was, as it were, "Gallican" even before the advent of Christianity. She continued to be Gallican, without any protest from Rome, up to the 9th and even the 11th century. She has remained instinctively Gallican to a certain extent even today. The Council of Chelles,[16] under Robert the Pious, declared as follows: *placuit sanciri, si quid a Papa Romano contra patrum decreta suggeretur, cassum et irritum fieri*: ". . . if aught should be put forward by the Pope of Rome contrary to the decrees of the Fathers of the Church, it shall be held null and void." The unifying work of the "ultramontane" monks of Cluny, however useful from certain points of view, nevertheless ultimately destroyed the rich and varied forms of worship that had developed on the soil of Gaul: the splendour of the Gallican liturgy, devotional practices dating from the first centuries, local traditions and cults. In effect, it amounted to a second Roman conquest, religious this time.[17]

The final "Latin" conquest—a secular one—took place in the field of literature towards the end of the 16th C. The language was refashioned according to classical models and, in the process, impoverished, losing its primitive savour. Rabelais was perhaps the last *gaulois* in French literature—someone who knew how to combine a love of classical authors (Greek above all) with a faithfulness to the spirit of his native soil.

The idea—pernicious because abstract—the myth that pretends that France is a "Latin" country, took hold of people's minds little by little. Yet this myth of a "Latin culture" has no more validity than the "pure race" mythology of the Germans, which was invented in Prussia—a country formed, ironically, by a mixture of Baltic, Slav, and Finno-Mongolian tribes, under a thin layer of Teutonic conquerors.

---

[16]Near Meaux, held in 993 or 994.

[17]Cluny (northwest of Lyons) was founded in 909 as a centre of spiritual reform and renewal, observing the Benedictine rule with a strictness unusual at the time. Many monasteries then were dominated by a nearby king or nobleman. The intention was that Cluny, by contrast, should be independent of all but papal jurisdiction.

The only difference is that this Latin myth embraces more of a literary, philological aspect, whereas today's Germanic myth prefers a semblance of science, the physiological. Will we ever learn to free ourselves from this abstract myth of "the unity of the Latin world"? Will the aggressive stance of our "Latin sister", faithful ally of the Germans, teach us something in this respect?[18]

Behind us, near Orléans, black clouds were gathering. We quickened our pace. The sky clouded over and it began to rain, so that we had to seek shelter in the undergrowth, among the bushes. I began to grumble about this absurd and unexpected impediment, which was delaying our progress. But almost at once I had to admit that this storm—which had forced me to leave the highway, exposed as it was to the heavens—was, in fact, a providential and salutary stroke of luck. Two terrifying explosions could be heard quite nearby. Two bombs had landed in the forest. At the same time, the chatter of machine-guns and the deafening drone of aeroplanes—quite close and coming straight at me—forced me to throw myself face down on the ground. Instinctively, I covered my head with my haversack—"like an ostrich", I thought to myself as I lay there. They passed over like a hurricane, skimming the treetops, ten metres or so above me. Two minutes later I got to my feet again, intending to come out of my hiding place, when a soldier shouted out, "Take cover! They'll be back. They've spotted us!" The planes flew over us three or four times in this way, strafing the bushes at random. Rabbits, frightened by the bombs, were leaving the forest. Then I saw an animal that at first I mistook for an Alsatian. Tall, with slender paws, its fur a strange greyish white colour, its mouth powerful and vicious-looking, its tail drooping . . . A wolf . . . quite simply, a wolf! Poor companion in misfortune, hunted down by the selfsame danger . . .

When I did finally get back onto the highway, the bombers were far off, heading back towards Orléans. The doleful sound of a distant air-raid siren could be heard. A long way off, bombs were falling again. Thanks to the rain, I don't think anyone in our group had been wounded

[18]The reference is to Italy, which in May 1939 had signed the "Pact of Steel" with the Nazis. Three days before Lossky left Paris, she had declared war on France (and Britain).

or hit. At least, this time I didn't see any corpses or anyone wounded—although a fellow traveller told me later that he had seen the twisted body of a young man under a tree, next to his bicycle, a bullet-hole in his forehead. Perhaps there were others like him, still in the bushes . . .

I wanted to reach La-Ferté-Saint-Aubin before nightfall, so I had to find a lift. Eventually, a military truck stopped for me. I sat down next to several young men. One of them, who was wearing a helmet, stared at me, dumbstruck. I gave a cry of surprise: it was the young companion with whom I had set off from Paris two days earlier and whom I had left at Brétigny yesterday morning. Sometimes the open road does hold in store for us such surprises.

He told me how, along with other recruits, he had boarded a train reserved for them going to Étampes, where he had no doubt arrived at the same time as myself. The train had been bombed and machine-gunned *en route*. Then they had marched from Étampes until being picked up by this truck.

I hardly recognised the young man, normally so timid and gauche. The helmet he had found somewhere along the way gave him a decidedly martial air. He was cheerful and relaxed, with the air of a real soldier of fortune, a devil-may-care old campaigner content with his lot. Along with his companions, he was to report to the military authorities at a place of their choosing.

The truck made slow progress. A few kilometres before La-Ferté-Saint-Aubin it stopped in the middle of nowhere. It was pitch dark. We were to spend the night there, under the stars or, rather, in the rain that was just beginning to fall. I spread my blanket out on the sodden grass, used my knapsack as a pillow, and covered myself with my coat. Water trickled over the edges. We could hear the drone of German planes somewhere or other. We heard them dropping their strings of bombs in the distance, on the railway line no doubt. The soldiers woke and loaded their rifles; then, deciding that the enemy was far off, went back to sleep again. We slept well. You can get used to anything.

DAY 4

Sunday 16th June

We set off again quite early. The truck was now going at a good speed. Numbed by our sodden clothes, we were happy all the same to be racing along in the morning sun. The young lads were singing their heads off.

We made a brief halt by a stream. What a delight to give our faces a quick splash among the reeds in the green, muddy water! At Lamotte-Beuvron everyone made a dash for the nearest grocery store. There was quite a queue and you had to wait a long time before being able to buy so much as a tin of food or a bar of chocolate. We managed to get a regional newspaper, from which we learned that the Germans had got further than Paris and were continuing their thrust towards the Loire. Somewhere near Rheims they had successfully made a breach in our defences and were skirting round the Maginot line. Faces fell. The cheerfulness of the young recruits fizzled out. The soldiers muttered threats and curses against "the traitors" . . . .

By the time we reached Vierzon, the sun was beating down. For the second time, I bade farewell to my young, helmeted companion. The truck was bound for Toulouse and he had decided to travel further, at a venture. As for me, I sought out the *gendarmerie* with a firm resolve to sort out my situation once and for all.

At the *gendarmerie* no one had any time to be bothered with me. "Come back in a few days," they said. "But," I protested, "where am I supposed to spend these few days?" "Well, go and try to find accommodation with relatives or friends and then report to the nearest *gendarmerie*. Anyway, the entire *département* is being evacuated. You'll just have to fend for yourself."

Things suddenly became very clear: what I should do was rejoin my family. They had been evacuated from Paris ten days earlier, to

51

Chabris in the Indre. My Iliad was turning into an Odyssey. I had the vague feeling that Chabris-sur-Cher was not far from Vierzon and that a series of coincidences had been leading me, from one *gendarmerie* to another, towards the very place where my family ought to be. My route to the army was becoming a path homewards.

I needed to get hold of a map, at all costs. But it was Sunday, the shops were closed and, to top it all, Vierzon was in the process of being evacuated. It had just been bombed—that very morning, or the evening before. The planes had aimed at the bridges most of all, and one had suffered damage. There were two gaping holes in the cobblestones, but the old stone structure was holding up and troops were still able to pass over it. Armoured cars as well, towing heavy cannons.

An atmosphere of unease pervaded the place. I thought that perhaps my family, too—carried along by this general tide of migration—had left Chabris to seek refuge further south. However, I did have friends there, whom I had known in Paris. Perhaps I would be able to track them down so as to enquire about what had happened to my wife and children. Eventually, in a small café, I managed to find someone with a local map. Chabris was only 35 kilometres away, on the road to Tours!

The road followed the right bank of the River Cher, or rather the Canal du Berry,[1] and was lined with poplars. The fresh, smiling greenery, the plentiful clear waters, and the clusters of tall trees all put me in mind of neighbouring Touraine.

It was to these provinces—Berry, Touraine and Anjou—that French royalty had repaired at what was perhaps the most tragic moment in its history: it was at Chinon that Charles VII, the "King of Bourges", had received the Maid of Orleans. Thereafter it was in these provinces that the kings had established their residences for more than a century: Louis XI at Plessis-les-Tours, Charles VIII at Amboise, Louis XII at Blois, François I at Chambord. It was from here too that they had set about the task of unifying France. And now, this same region—royal par excellence—was in danger. The dull sound of

---

[1]The canal runs alongside the river.

aircraft could be heard, high in the sky. Ten German bombers were heading for Blois and Tours.

As for the kings, no one—not even a diehard republican—can deny that it was they who established French unity. It should never be forgotten that, long before it became a Republic, France was a King-dom, one whose traditions date back to the time of Clovis. All of the faults and errors of the Ancien Régime put together cannot erase this tradition of a "royal" France. To pretend otherwise, to pretend that "France" began in 1789, would mean striking from the pages of his-tory thirteen centuries both majestic and tragic, filled with glory and grief, triumphs and toil. No, its institutions may change, but France remains the same—with its tradition of royalty even under the Repub-lic, and its spirit of democracy even under the Ancien Régime. It is a country of liberty—in the moral sense of the word. A sense more pro-found than all the political and social "freedoms" coveted by the var-ious parties. For it is an inner liberty, a heroic ability to renew oneself, to hold one's head up high, while rejecting from one's being anything that smacks of decay or death, anything that tends to become "ancien régime" in the bad sense. A true royalist cannot be conservative.

Nor is it possible to deny the wild grandeur of revolutionary France—the France of Danton and Carnot, which was able to stand up to the whole of Europe in the matter of arms. Valmy, Jemmapes, and Toulon were French victories just as much as were Bouvines, Orléans, and Marignan.[2] Nonetheless, revolutionaries are always in the wrong since, in their juvenile fervour for everything new, in their

---

[2]The first three were victories won by the French Revolutionary Army—two in 1792, the third in 1793—against the Prussians, the Austrians and the British, respec-tively. Valmy ensured the survival of the Revolution, while Toulon marked the last external attempt to defeat it. The second group of victories were more widely spread in time. Bouvines (1214) is thought of as "the battle that made France"; France's very existence is credited to Philippe II's decisive victory there. The Siege of Orléans (1428–9) proved a turning-point in the Hundred Years' War and was the first major French success since the defeat at Agincourt. At Marignan (1515), François I defeated the Swiss, who had until then acquired the reputation of being invincible. The victory—won at the dawn of François' reign and the beginning of the French Renaissance—achieved symbolic status, evoking that other great leader, Caesar—who was himself one of the few ever to have beaten the Swiss.

hopes for a better future and a way of life built on justice, they always base themselves on theories that are abstract and artificial, making a clean sweep of living tradition which is, after all, founded on the experience of centuries.

Conservatives are always wrong, too, despite being rich in life experience, despite being shrewd and prudent, intelligent and sceptical. For, in their desire to preserve ancient institutions that have withstood the test of time, they decry the necessity of renewal, and man's yearning for a better way of life.

Both attitudes carry within themselves the seeds of death. Is there, then, a third way? Another destiny for society than of always being subject to the threat of revolutions which destroy life, or reactionary attitudes which mummify it? Or is this the inevitable fate of all terrestrial cities, the natural law of their existence?

In fact, only in the Church can we find both a Tradition that knows no revolution and at the same time the impetus towards a new life that has no end. [3] Her "theory" (understood in the true sense of the word, namely "vision"[4]) is based on a constant experience of Truth. Which is why she is in possession of those infinite resources upon which may draw all who are called to govern the perishable cities of this world.

Will we ever learn to maintain the correct balance between that which is God's and that which is Caesar's?

France—"elder daughter of the Church", with her ancient tradition of Gallicanism that was defended by her kings—knew how to do justice to the Church's spiritual prerogatives while at the same time firmly opposing any interference by the ecclesiastical powers in the internal affairs of the kingdom. In the conflict between the *sacer-*

---

[3]Lossky would later write more than once on *Tradition* (which he saw as being essentially the life of the Holy Spirit within the Church) and the difference between it and *traditions*. Most memorably and powerfully, perhaps, in his essay "Tradition and Traditions", which is included in *In the Image and Likeness of God* and also in *The Meaning of Icons*.

[4]Lossky's juxtaposition of the words 'vision' and 'theory' surely anticipates the lectures he was to give but a few years later (1945–46) on 'La Vision de Dieu'. These were published posthumously in 1962 as Vision de Dieu (Delachaux & Niestlé) and translated as *The Vision of God* (The Faith Press, 1963). The text refers *passim* to the Greek word θεωρία, meaning "vision" or "contemplation".

dotium and the *imperium*, she defended the cause of the Church against that of a "Holy" Empire. Yet her position was crystal clear: "The King of France is Emperor in his Kingdom".[5] Nevertheless, each time a king assumed the actual title of "emperor"—driven by the magical power that attaches itself to words—the balance was lost.

The Empire of Charlemagne, for example, created a strange confusion between the spiritual and the temporal. Bishops controlled the administrative tasks of counts, while counts busied themselves with matters diocesan. Councils drew up capitularies,[6] while assemblies of grandees dictated canons. The royal court, grouped round the Imperial Chapel [7] and, seized with theological fervour, sought to ensure the triumph of a novel teaching concerning the procession of the Holy Spirit. Pressure from the Frankish empire caused this strange teaching to triumph in the West. After resisting for a while, the Popes were in the end obliged to alter the traditional, sacred text of the Creed.[8] From then on, schism from the Eastern Patriarchates became inevitable. (Byzantium, on the other hand, never experienced such an extreme case of Caesaropapism.)

In this unhealthy, confused atmosphere the Empire infused into the Church the venom of secular domination. During the papacy of Gregory VII (Hildebrand)—a German intoxicated by the dream of a world empire—the "unfortunate Donation of Constantine" deplored

[5]"*Le roi de France est empereur en son royaume*": the phrase quoted by Lossky—much used in the 13th C—is well known to any student of French history. It epitomised the belief that the king was supreme in his kingdom, above and beyond any feudal relationships. But also that he had no desire to extend his "empire" beyond the bounds of his kingdom—unlike the Germanic Emperor. In addition, the motto conveyed the belief that the French king was not subordinate to such an emperor—nor indeed to the Pope.

[6]A *capitulary* was a series of legislative or administrative acts emanating from the Frankish courts of the Merovingian and Carolingian dynasties, especially that of the first emperor, Charlemagne.

[7]The Palatine Chapel in Aachen (Aix-la-Chapelle) is the chapel of Charlemagne's palace, and now part of Aachen Cathedral. It contains his remains and was the site of coronations for 600 years.

[8]Lossky is referring, of course, to the insertion into the Creed of the phrase *filioque*, and the associated belief that the Holy Spirit proceeds from the Father "*and from the Son*".

by Dante ceased to be a phantom and became a reality.[9] France, on the other hand, having become an independent kingdom once again under the Capetians, rediscovered a *via media* and the wise moderation of its traditional Gallicanism.

Saint Louis, for example, knew well enough how to distinguish between the roles of administrator of justice and defender of the Church, as the following incident, related by Joinville, clearly shows:

I saw the king on another occasion, at a time when all the French prelates had said they wished to speak with him, and he had gone to his palace to hear what they had to say. Bishop Guy of Auxerre, the son of Guillaume de Mello, was among those present, and he addressed the king on behalf of all the prelates. 'Your Majesty,' he said, 'the Lords Spiritual of this realm here present have directed me to tell you that the cause of Christianity, which it is your duty to guard and defend, is being ruined in your hands.' On hearing these words the king crossed himself and said: 'Pray tell me how that may be'.

"Your Majesty," said the bishop, "it is because at the present time excommunications are so lightly regarded that people think nothing of dying without seeking absolution, and refuse to make their peace with the Church. The Lords Spiritual require you therefore, for the love of God and because it is your duty, to command your provosts and your bailiffs to seek out all those who allow themselves to remain under the ban of the Church for a year

---

[9]See *Inferno* XIX:115–7. "Ah, Constantine! to how much ill gave birth,/ Not thy conversion, but that plenteous dower/ Which the first wealthy Father gain'd from thee" (Tr. by H.F.Cary; J.M.Dent 1908). Dante had already discussed the issue in *De Monarchia* Bk. 2.

Constantine, Emperor 306–337, transferred the seat of Empire to Byzantium donating (so it was believed in the Middle Ages) the western part of the Empire to the Pope. The "Donation of Constantine" was the document in which this supposed fact was recorded and which thus became pivotal in establishing the temporal power of the Papacy. In the 15th century, it was proved to be a forgery, probably dating from the 8th or 9th century.

Hildebrand was not, in fact, German but Italian, having been born in Tuscany, though as a young man he did reside and study in Germany. He was Pope from 1073 to 1085.

and a day, and compel them, by seizure of their possessions, to get themselves absolved."

The king replied that he would willingly give such orders provided he himself could be shown without any doubt that the persons concerned were in the wrong. The bishop told him that the prelates would not on any account accept this condition, since they questioned his right to adjudicate in their affairs. The king replied that he would not do anything other than he had said; for it would be against God and contrary to right and justice if he compelled any man to seek absolution when the clergy were doing him wrong. [. . .] So the prelates resigned themselves to accepting things as they were; and I have never heard tell that any further demand was made in relation to this matter. [10]

I watched the German planes as they flew towards the royal region of Touraine. The road was long and I began to despair of reaching my destination before nightfall. However, obligingly and as if in answer to my prayers, a truck pulled up. An old peasant woman and her young daughter invited me to climb aboard. The daughter was a cheerful soul, blessed with the kind of gaiety that comes from the fields and the fresh air of the open countryside. They were on their way home . . . to Chabris. What a stroke of luck! I settled down beside a plough on the back of the truck and we set off through fields and meadows bathed in the evening sun.

[10]Jean de Joinville (c.1224–1317) was one of the great chroniclers of mediaeval France. A pious man, he was concerned with the proper administration of the kingdom. In 1244 when King Louis IX (the future Saint Louis) organised the 7th Crusade, Joinville decided to follow his King, becoming his close friend, counsellor and confidant, particularly during the four years they spent together in the Holy Land after the failure of the venture. During Louis' canonisation process (successfully concluded in 1297), Joinville's testimony was invaluable. He himself died some 50 years after the death of Louis, aged 93. It was in 1309, at the request of Queen Jeanne de Navarre, that he had begun work on his *Histoire de Saint Louis*. Lossky's quotation is from Ch. CXXXV, the section headed *"Il repousse une demande injuste des évêques"*. The translation used is by M.R.B. Shaw: 'The Life of Saint Louis' in *Joinville and Ville-hardouin: Chronicles of the Crusades* (Penguin Classics, 1963), pp.177–8).

We chatted merrily as we went along and I suddenly felt enveloped by an atmosphere of peace and well-being that was as yet uncontaminated by the horrors of war. The two women exchanged gossip about various agricultural tasks, or else about little facts and details to do with the life of the *canton*. The war still hadn't affected their lives. They were living in quite another world. In fact, could this or any war ever destroy the hardworking, healthy way of life of the French countryside? All through the Hundred Years' War peasants had continued to till the land, to hoe, to make hay, to bring in the harvest. For the earth—always demanding of those who cultivate it—has no wish to hear of wars or truces. In the company of these two peasants and for the first time since leaving Paris, I felt embarrassed about my forbidding appearance. I must have looked like a lame tramp in my dirty, dusty clothes and my four days' growth of beard.

When I got to Chabris, my family was nowhere to be found. Apparently, they had left a few days earlier, making for the *département* of the Lot, much further south. I took a room in the hotel, shaved, washed carefully for the first time, and went to pay a visit to my old friends from Paris, who had stayed on.[11]

The sound of anti-aircraft fire could be heard not far off. The locals stopped what they were doing to look at the spectacle, as three German planes circled high in the sky, pursued by our fighters. Small black clouds formed around the planes, becoming more and more numerous. Suddenly one plane turned upside down, jolted, rolled over and over in an attempt to right itself, then nose-dived at an ever increasing speed, like a skylark falling onto a cornfield.

The sight of towns being bombed is painful and depressing, but watching a battle such as this gladdens the heart and gives one a feeling of youthful courage, noble and steadfast in the face of death.

My friends were greatly surprised to see me. For my part, I was pleased suddenly to find myself among people I knew, seated on a

[11]Alexandre Ougrimov, head of the Résistance at Dourdan, was deported from France in 1947 (as part of retaliatory measures taken by the Government) and spent 8 years in a Gulag camp (with Solzhenitsyn). He died in Moscow in 1981. His wife, Irène, went to join him in Russia of her own free will. She too spent 8 years in a Gulag camp. She died in Moscow in 1994. [*Original editor's note.*]

chair with a bowl of steaming soup in front of me, in a peaceful, family atmosphere. It was as if I were a ghost come back from the gloomy depths of Hades to tell the living all about the horrors met with along the infernal road.

Learning that a train for Le Blanc would be leaving the following morning, I decided to take it. It would at least mean 100 kilometres less to travel on foot. Back at the hotel, I was at long last able to lie in a real bed, with white sheets, under a decent blanket. The little town slept peacefully. All that could be heard was the barking of dogs and, from the old church across the way, the sound of its clock striking the hours of the night.

Monday 17th June

After breakfasting *en famille*, I set off for the station, accompanied by my friend. The train for Le Blanc finally arrived, an hour late. I had to fight my way into one of the cattle trucks, since the refugees who were already squashed up inside—some sitting, some standing—were determined that no more people should be allowed in. Several of the third-class carriages had been reserved for the wounded from a hospital at Romorantin which was being evacuated. This rail journey of 100 kilometres proved to be, if not the saddest episode of my entire journey, certainly the most tedious. The train kept stopping, shunting, and coming to a complete standstill.

At Valençay, it stopped for three hours. I was torn between the fear of losing my place and the wish to visit the château, which could be seen in the distance, with its degenerate, harmless towers in the Renaissance style.[1] Prowling about on the platform, I got into conversation with my travelling companions. One soldier, who had been wounded in the face ten days earlier by a bomb dropped somewhere in the *département de l'Oise*, told me of his misfortunes which, in fact, were common to us all. "Ah, *mon vieux*," he added, "if only we had had enough equipment, we could have held out!" A Polish refugee told me of the horrors of the war in his own country, about its fiercely fought defence in which he had taken part as an officer. He described the horrifying struggle, in which both sides gave up taking prisoners, simply killing captives instead. After his first exodus last September, he was now having to make a second, within France. "Because," he

---

[1] A 12th C castle was demolished to make way for this huge château with its false battlements and outsized, domed towers that are of no defensive value. Hence Lossky's colourful use of the adjective 'degenerate'.

explained, "the Germans won't spare us Poles. They look on us as their subjects." He told me how, during an air raid, a woman he knew who was travelling on the road with him, suddenly lost her mind. She had to be interned in a lunatic asylum at Romorantin. Her 15-year-old son had had to carry on alone, abandoning his mother. Perhaps for ever.

Other sorrowful tales were told, together forming a chorus of lamentation similar to those in the tragedies of Euripides. Verses from the Apocalypse came to mind, the ones describing vast multitudes made up of all the peoples and tribes of the earth, dressed in white— "they which come out of the great tribulation"—whose every tear God Himself would wipe away.[2] Yet, do people still know—do *we* still know—the value of suffering, so that instead of hardening our hearts it might open within us a source of new life?

A newspaper was passed round. A new cabinet had just been formed, under the presidency of Marshal Pétain.

The train set off once more, and then stopped again. Exasperated and at their wits' end, the refugees were seized with panic each time the sound of a plane—even a French one—was heard. Piled up against each other, sometimes sitting, sometimes standing so as to give our stiff legs a rest, we were all but suffocated by the heat and the fetid air. There was to be ten hours of this torture.

In the train were people of all sorts, of every tongue and nation: Belgians, Poles, Russians, Spaniards, Greeks, Moroccans, Africans. The confusion of Babel? Or the miracle of Pentecost? Both interpretations were possible. For the moment, one thing is clear: just as during the period of the "great migrations" towards the end of the Roman Empire and the birth of a new Europe, so now we are living at a time of different "diasporas", with heterogeneous peoples mingling and mixing.

Rome, with its rigid, narrow-minded Latin ethos, fell; whereas the Hellenic suppleness of Byzantium was able to triumph over the barbarians. Constantinople—that "Paris of the Middle Ages"—became a focus of culture, spirituality and political education for the new

[2]Cf. Apocalypse 7:9–17.

states that were developing under its tutelage. Alone in the West, Gaul was able to maintain its unity, to rebuild itself, knowing how to make use of new ethnic and cultural elements, how to fuse these disparate yet juxtaposed components in its powerful melting-pot and to make them her own, renewing the national organism. Of all the colonies of Sarmantes and Alains, the only trace that survives today are the place-names Sermaine and Alainville. The Burgunds became Burgundians, the Scandinavians who settled in Neustria became Normans, the Orientals from the Mediterranean gave to the Midi its own particular charm. And all became genuinely French, sons of the same spiritual family, of a homeland that continually renewed itself by absorbing newcomers. Camille Jullian, in his admirable study of the historical origins of France that is so full of hope for the future, was right when he observed:

> For the land known as France to have come into being and for us to have become French men and women, a long-drawn-out human undertaking was necessary. It began the first day men appeared on our soil and has continued without interruption since then. No one can affirm that this process has been completed or that the centuries to come will not contribute some new characteristic to the features of France, some form of unexpected wealth to her terrain, or one more task to her national life. For I am among those who believe that, however long it took in the past for her formation, the destiny of France is only just beginning.[3]

I don't know where the fashionable opinion comes from—in fact, it has become a commonplace—that divides humanity up into "old nations", who are destined for degeneration and historical death, and "young nations", called to supplant the "old" and to take their place. Probably, the origin of this way of thinking is the clumsy application

---

[3]Camille Jullian (1859–1933) was a historian, philologist and archaeologist who specialised in Gaul and the Roman epoch. Professor of national antiquities at the Collège de France, he was elected to the Académie des Inscriptions et Belles-Lettres in 1908 and to the Académie française in 1924. Lossky is quoting from a paragraph found on p. 9 of Jullian's *De la Gaule à la France. Nos origines historiques* (Hachette, 1922).

of the laws of biology to the domain of sociology. A case of an organic theory being stretched too far. For, though it is possible to draw an analogy between an animal organism and the body of a nation, it remains nevertheless an analogy. That is, a comparison of limited validity between two different categories, between two essentially unrelated phenomena. If this were not so, it would be a case, not of analogy but equivalence. The "organism" of a nation does not belong to the realm of biology, any more than the composition of an animal body falls within the province of mineralogy, even though one can perhaps find some points that it has in common with the structure of a crystal. Again, one may agree with Aristotle and modern vitalists that animal organisms have an entelechy—*i.e.* an ordering, creative force which governs the body's formation, growth and maturity only to lose all control over it little by little, becoming a powerless onlooker of the organic form's destruction. However, is there really a similar "entelechy" governing the destiny of a given people, with its periods of grandeur and decadence?

In the history of any nation, there enters into play a new factor, one unknown to the sciences called "exact"—namely, free will. The "soul" of a people is not some being superior to individuals that determines their actions, transforming them into mere vital functions of an organism in the manner of an entelechy that organizes the functioning of cells in a body. Our role is immeasurably greater, our responsibility without limits. For the true soul of a people is made up of our acts of heroism and our moments of cowardice, our righteous actions and our sins, our deeds in favour of life and those favouring death. Formed by millions of free wills, governed by the divine will, helped along by the saints—who walk in God's ways and watch over their people—this soul of a people, this non-organic, so-called "entelechy" is always in the process of being formed, always in the process of becoming, always dependent on our acts and decisions. It is called historical destiny.

That France should be able to renew its "national organism" by absorbing new elements, without ceasing to remain the same France, continuing the same tradition, tracing the same destiny on the pages of history—this seems indisputable. But in order to assimilate foreign cultures, one must understand them, comprehend them from within. Otherwise the newcomers will always remain "aliens", keeping their hereditary mind-sets under the external appearances of being French, adding their vices to our faults. In order to absorb, the soul must expand; contraction is always a sign of death.

The gift of tongues at Pentecost, which transformed a few dozen sons of the historical, physical Israel into the universal Church, was not simply a miraculous ability to speak foreign languages, but above all an infinite expansion of that nation's soul so as to render it capable of laying hold of the souls of all peoples, making them "prisoners of Christ".[4] Christian universalism has nothing to do with a cultural universalism, even when a given culture is Christianised. To confuse the two universalisms, to wish to substitute one for the other—Latin culture for that of the Church, for example—is to expose this church to the cruel blows of fate. The first such was struck by the schism from the East; the second by the Reformation, the schism of the Germanic world from Rome.

True, France did follow the religious destiny of the Latin world, but she still keeps deeply rooted within her being the latent tradition of Gallicanism. In the widest sense of the word, Gallicanism is nothing other than the defence of the rights of one local church, autonomous in its interior life, faithful to its ancient traditions of ancient piety and the Christian culture particular to it. It is at the same time a universalism, but a concrete one based on the rich diversity of Christian territories each guarding its traditions; on a multiplicity of local churches, different from each other yet at the same time forming the One, Holy, Catholic and Apostolic Church. For the mystery of catholicity lies in a unity which is diverse. There can be no local catholicity just as there is no abstract catholicity above and beyond local traditions. The primacy of one Patriarchal See over the others does not mean that one local church can impose upon the others its own traditions, as if they were universal. This has been the error of Latinism.

France has not been immune from making this mistake. She did so whenever, in a secular context, she wished to lend her national culture

[4] Cf. Ephesians 3:1.

an abstract, universal character. The Declaration of the Rights of Man and of the Citizen that the Revolution sought to impose on the world—was it not the expression of a false catholicity, a bastardised Latinisim? It was certainly a renunciation of Gallican *juste mesure* and was the reason why the Revolution ended up as an Empire with global pretensions.

To rediscover this *juste mesure*, this *via media*, in all its fullness so as to activate this Gallicanism which has so far remained a latent instinct—perhaps this is France's religious mission. A mission full of promise, for it would ensure that France had, not simply the spiritual capacity necessary to absorb foreign elements, but also a strength and inner dynamism, whose source can only be religious. Faced with Latin Christianity and its tendency to abstractions, to homogenisation and sterilisation; faced with a pagan and only too concrete Pan-Germanism founded on a mystique of "blood and soil" that seeks to refashion the world according to its creed, France could then become a focus of regeneration for Western Christianity in a Europe that is becoming de-Christianised. She could become a land of a new Christian mission, the land of those "Apostles of the Last Times" announced by the Holy Virgin to Mélanie on the hilltop at La Salette.[5]

The train arrived at Le Blanc towards evening. This slow, tiresome journey was finally at an end. I enquired about trains to Limoges. No, there would be no more trains until further orders. I would have to continue on foot again. More than 200 kilometres to go. Four or five days' walking, unless I managed to find a lift along the way.

While waiting, I went to the reception centre. In a room in the town hall, refugees were crowding round some tables, awaiting their turn to be given a bowl of soup, some bread, or—for the children—a cup of chocolate. Others stayed outside, sitting on the steps or on the ground. Where were all these people going to be accommodated? This thought caused me to rush out of the room and to walk straight through the town, wanting to leave Le Blanc behind before darkness

---

[5]Mélanie Calvat was the elder of the two shepherd children who were reported to have seen the Virgin Mary (the other being Maximin Giraud).

fell. I planned to spend the night in a barn somewhere, bathed in the fresh air of the countryside.

I crossed over the River Creuse and came to the upper town on its rocky mound overlooking the river. The towers of the château and the ancient steeples stood out against the verdant evening sky. The waters of the Creuse looked greenish, too. Huge military trucks crossed the bridge one after another, then continued uphill following the left bank. The locals watched them go by, sitting peacefully outside their doors, enjoying the evening calm. I was in a peaceful zone, at last, where towns did not seem to be in a process of evacuation. In a small inn I was given some red wine and a hunk of white bread. I would have to get a move on if I were not to be caught out by nightfall. As I climbed out of the town, I was joined by a young cyclist who was having to push his bike up the incline. As we walked along together, I discovered that, like me, he had fled the reception centre and was looking for a barn out in the countryside.

We were given shelter by an old farmer, as talkative as he was kind. His barn was as spacious as a palace, one of the old-style, sturdy and solid, with the lofty structure typical of the Berry region. It had seen several generations of peasants come and go.

After chatting with the old man for a long while in the moonlit courtyard, we went off to sleep in the hay.

Tuesday June 18th

The sky was dull. A fine rain was falling, as gentle as dew, the sort of rain that seems to want to go on for ever, interminably. The horizon was shrouded in a pearly grey mist. Resigning myself to the fact that I would be soaked to the skin within an hour, I set off in the direction of Bellac, on the Limoges road. However, a corporal gave me a lift as far as La Trimouille. No great distance, but another ten kilometres under my belt nonetheless.

A bowl of hot broth revived me. The little inn at La Trimouille was packed with some thirty *poilus*. In spite of the defeat, in spite of the journey into the unknown that they were now embarked upon, in spite of the rain, they were carefree and gay. Walking up and down between the tables, a lieutenant watched his men as they ate. "Come on, lads," he said with a good-natured smile. "Get a move on! We've got to be on our way again." This atmosphere of camaraderie, this virile and healthy army atmosphere aroused in me a longing for barrack-room life.

A few kilometres further along the road, I got a lift in a truck going to Bellac. No question that my luck was in today! My companions this time were a young woman with a baby, a refugee from Valenciennes, and a soldier rejoining his company somewhere or other in the region. The soldier was telling me about Dunkirk. A wall of fire on land, a rain of missiles at sea. Bombs and torpedoes had fallen on all sides of the vessel that transported the troops he was with over to England. "We were scared stiff! . . . I don't like the English much," he added, "but after the warm welcome they gave us, they've gone up a bit in my estimation. Because I've got to admit that we were treated like royalty. And then after a week's rest, we were thrown back into the furnace. We had a narrow escape, alright!"

The young woman told us of some news she had heard that very morning. Russia had apparently declared war on Germany. But was it true? A similar rumour had been rife in Paris, two days before my departure. Hopes had been raised for a while. We had been only too willing to hold out for just a little while longer, for we thought we were on the eve of a new Miracle of the Marne.[1] Our disappointment had been all the greater, when we learned that the news had been false.

A Franco-Russian alliance has always been a historical necessity for both countries. It is imperative, in the manner of a natural understanding between those who, although they have nothing to share, nothing to provoke reciprocal covetous desires, yet have everything to defend against common adversaries. The communist danger? Well, look at Richelieu. He certainly knew how to triumph over the Huguenots at home, while at the same time relying on Protestant nations in his foreign policy against Catholic Austria and the Papal States.[2] Then again, during this general crisis that we are living through, it is not from the degenerate communism of the Russians that we have the most to fear. Did we not seek an alliance from this same communist Russia a year ago? Then, she preferred to ally herself with Germany—our enemy, but also her own natural enemy. Was this a betrayal? One can only betray those to whom one is bound by obligation. Anyone wishing to speak of betrayal must look for it elsewhere. The Treaty of Munich, it must frankly be admitted, was itself nothing but a betrayal, a renunciation of our obligations towards those countries of Central Europe threatened with war. It might be objected that, in September 1938, we were not prepared for war. Well, we were no more prepared today, alas! In fact, it was this same Treaty

[1]The 'Miracle of the Marne' is a popular way of referring to the First Battle of the Marne (September 1914). In August the entire Allied army on the Western Front was in retreat. It seemed that Paris would be taken, as the French and British fell back towards the River Marne. When they seized on a German tactical error, however, the tables were 'miraculously' turned.

[2]Cardinal de Richelieu—Louis XIII's Chief Minister from 1624 until his death in 1642—was, despite the caricature of him in such books as *The Three Musketeers*, one of the greatest politicians in French history. He is generally credited with having freed France from its feudal nature, turning it into a unified state, and with helping it become the leading power in Europe. He also founded the *Académie française*.

of Munich that pushed Russia into its alliance with Germany, its enemy, so as to avoid the *Drang nach Osten*, the Drive towards the East, of which Hitler dreamed and which the rest of Europe would have witnessed with indifference. The Soviets avoided this danger; but the weapons prepared against Russia were turned on us, with the result that armour-plated hordes invaded the West.

Right now, however, it isn't a question of looking for earlier mistakes. They would form a long list that could well extend far back into the past. France needs now to do just one thing: to learn to pull herself up, to maintain and increase her inner strength so as not to be crushed by her misfortunes, and to be able courageously to confront the imminent catastrophe. As for this catastrophe, who can save us from it? England? . . . America? . . . Russia? . . . No one except God. God alone. For the interconnected sequence of our faults does indeed extend back very far, even as far back as the sin of Adam. Yet this chain, this horizontal line that we call history, was broken at a given moment more than 1,900 years ago by another line, one that was vertical. God became Man, descending even to the infernal abyss so as to give us the power to escape from this interminable chain of faults and to rise above history. The intersection of these two lines forms the shape of the Cross. By accepting our historical catastrophe in all its horror, as our own cross given to us by God, we will find a way out, the only way: the vertical line that leads up to God.[3]

By now we had left behind Le Dorat and its Romanesque church whose round side-chapels protrude from the main wall of the apse, so that from outside they resemble squat, sturdy towers. Clearly, we were now in Limousin, a region characterized by its Romanesque art and architecture. At Bellac I had to get down from the truck and continue on foot. But, determined to reach Limoges before evening, I began to look for another lift. In the town centre, a large motor coach was preparing to leave. I could see that there were still one or two empty seats, so I went up to it. When I saw the passengers, I felt like laughing: here were twenty or so pale-faced civil servants, sullen and full of a sense of their own dignity, themselves looking for all the world like

[3]This horizontal/vertical imagery would be developed in Lossky's later writings. For example, in the article "Tradition and Traditions", referred to on p. 54, note 3.

a pile of dusty old documents. Real pen-pushers from out of a comic film. "Any room for a *mobilisable* coming from Paris?" I asked. Twenty ill-tempered heads turned in my direction, answering in chorus like in a vaudeville, "No, no! There's no room! Not for anybody! This coach is for the Ministry. The Ministry's being evacuated. The Ministry, Monsieur! Do you work at the Ministry?" I burst out laughing and continued on my way.

Nonetheless, luck continued to favour me. A truck was slowly climbing the hill out of Bellac. The driver—a portly man with a good-humoured expression—motioned that I could climb onto the running-board. But the weight of my baggage and above all my right leg which was still causing me to limp prevented me from climbing up while walking. Just then, however, a car that had been following the truck stopped for me, so that this time I was able to climb onto the running-board. I clung onto the door, the wind whistling round my ears. We were going at a fair speed, still following the truck. It turned out that the two vehicles were travelling together, transporting a rather large family, along with its belongings. The truck was being driven by the father, a miller from Évrieux. The elder son was at the wheel of the car, in which two elderly women, two girls and a boy were sitting bunched up. Taking advantage of the convoy's first stop, I moved to the wider and more comfortable running-board of the truck. You could almost stretch out on it and have a sleep, if you wanted. The good miller and his family had no definite plan. They were just travelling straight ahead, to Limoges and further still, in the direction of Brive. For me, this was a stroke of extraordinary luck.

We got to Limoges at about four in the afternoon, just as a violent thunderstorm broke. It was followed by torrential rain. I hardly had time to drape my raincoat round my shoulders. Lightning struck quite close by. The deafeningly loud thunder seemed intent on crushing us. Still standing on the running-board, I remembered the aerial bombardments and rejoiced in the thought that this time I had at least fallen into "the hands of God" rather than "the hands of men". [4] Yet there was still the drawback of getting soaked to the skin by this

---

[4]Surely a reference, respectively, to Hebrews 10:31 and Matthew 17:22.

deluge, as the pouring rain fell thick and fast. The twisting streets of the town were transformed into torrents and the truck could make hardly any progress. The cathedral and the beautiful Romanesque churches loomed in turn through the greenish veil of rain.

Yet the sun soon began to break through the clouds, and a rainbow cast its bright colours behind us. The tarmac road glistened in the sun as it climbed through hills, wooded valleys and stony hillocks crowned by ruined châteaux. Still climbing, we went through La Pierre-Buffière, a small mediaeval market-town atop a hill, cramped and compact around its fortified castle, with its Romanesque church and ancient town-hall. The bells were ringing for the *Angelus*.[5]

It has often been claimed that the quintessential character of the typical French landscape lies in a harmonious relationship between nature and art; the former, profoundly "human", as though created for cultivation; the latter, ever "natural", a continuation of the work of God, a collaborating with Him in shaping the eternal countenance of France.

Yet there is another characteristic which makes France the most beautiful country on earth: a harmony in time, a continuity in the traditional way of life which takes the edges off the over-saliant angles of "modernism". In Paris the Eiffel Tower, for example, no longer shocks anyone save for a few snobs besotted by aestheticism. Nature, monuments, the easy way of life—all make up one perfect, living, immortal whole which cannot be split into past and present.

Compared to France, Italy is nothing but a museum where life vegetates in the shadow of the tombs of the past, overwhelmed by their majestic silence. Or else, gaudy and vulgar, it creates awful clashes, profaning old stones. I shall never forget the feeling of disappointment that took hold of me when I first visited Florence. I constantly had to make an effort to blot out the present in order to be able to admire the beauty of the past. As for Germany, what can one say? In this

---

[5]The *Angelus*—a devotion in memory of the Incarnation—takes its name from the opening words, *Angelus Domini nuntiavit Mariae*. It consists of three Biblical verses describing the mystery, alternating with the 'Hail Mary'. Traditionally it is recited three times a day—at 6.00 a.m., 12.00 noon and 6.00 p.m.—and is announced by the ringing of the Angelus bell.

country, the grandeur of the past has a sinister, ghostly character. Whereas the present is typified by a flat ugliness, harmoniousness being replaced by a pedantic symmetry. Nor is there any harmony between nature and civilisation. At times, nature has been entirely dominated by man, cut up into small uniform squares for agricultural exploitation, when it has not been totally obliterated by industrial landscapes. At other times, it throws up rocky terrain of wild, inhuman beauty, covered by fir-trees and inhabited by Rübezahl and other mischievous goblins.[6] France has never had any goblins. Her groves, hills and springs once sheltered wood-nymphs or Celtic fairies, those more "human" supernatural beings. Any dragons were definitively driven out by the disciples of the Apostles. The world of fairies eventually merged with heroic Christian legends so as to succour knights-errant in their perilous adventures.[7] Above all, however, the land was sanctified from the very first centuries by the blood of her martyrs and the constant prayers of her saints.

Such were the thoughts that came to mind as I contemplated the landscape of the central plateau that was now opening up before us: the Massif Central, sometimes called a *noyau de résistance*, a pocket of resistance.[8] Will it become tomorrow the land of our resistance against the enemy?[9] Or will French unity find support on another "massif", more "central" and more resistant still, one over which centuries of history have no hold? Namely, the traditions of Christian

[6]Rübezahl is a capricious mountain sprite of German folklore whose home is in the mountain range separating Prussian Silesia and Bohemia. Interestingly, the great Catholic poet and dramatist Paul Claudel—phrases from whose works are sometimes quoted by French-speaking Orthodox—wrote in similar vein in 1926: "Even as a child, I have always experienced the feeling of repulsion felt by most French minds at the fanciful goblins and elves that are so dear to the good folk of Germany." From the prose poem 'Mies', written in Japan during Claudel's time as Ambassador there and published in the volume *L'Oiseau noir dans le soleil levant* (1927).

[7]Lossky is alluding to mediaeval *Chansons de geste* such as *La Chanson de Roland* (see p. 42, n. 9) and to works by writers such as Chrétien de Troyes (12th C) who made use of the Arthurian legend with its *Chevaliers de la Table Ronde*.

[8]The allusion is both to the geography of the area and to the independent character of the inhabitants.

[9]Not long after these lines were penned, the French Resistance Movement did indeed come to have a particularly strong presence in the *Massif central*.

France, hardworking and faithful to its ancient soil that was made forever blessed by her saints. Invasions come and go, empires crumble. France will survive.

A new thunderstorm that rumbled ever closer forced us to halt for a while in a little hamlet a few kilometres from Masseret. As it turned out, we had to spend the night there. The miller and his family installed themselves in a barn, while I went to the inn, hoping to find a room where I could dry out my soaking wet clothes. In vain. Yet I did manage to get some piping hot soup, some wine and some cheese. The serving girl was terrified of the thunder and closed the windows and shutters. She seemed very worked up by the alarmist rumours spread by one of the guests. Sensing that panic was getting the better of her, she tried to cope with it by using *le mot de Cambronne* nonstop, left, right and centre.[10] Before long the person responsible for the rumours put in an appearance—a fat, flabby Flemish man. She turned to him and pointed at me, triumphantly. "There, you see! This gentleman has just come from Limoges and the *Boches* are *not* there yet. *Merde!*" Not seeming to be bothered by this observation, the man replied phlegmatically, "But they're evacuating the town". "You're mistaken," I said, irritated by his tone of certainty. "Well," he replied, "they've evacuated the aerodrome, anyway!" "But I've just come that way myself", I insisted, "and the planes are still there". He was unwilling to give in, however, and replied with the same composure. "I didn't mean airoplanes! I'm talking about aviation equipment." At this, everyone burst into laughter and the *mot de Cambronne* was repeated—along with several other expressions no less French, even though frowned upon by the *Dictionnaire de l'Académie*—in chorus this time, by our audience of a sergeant and four soldiers. The man had no option but to retire. As he left the room, our hostess joked, "If he weren't so stupid, I might have believed he was a fifth columnist."

We went off to sleep in the barn. You had to climb high up, right under the rafters. The hay was damp, the roof leaked. The man

---

[10]*Le mot de Cambronne*: this euphemism for the word *merde* takes its name from General Cambronne, commander of the Imperial Guard. Although entirely apocryphal, the popular story is that he uttered it after the Battle of Waterloo, when asked by the English to surrender.

sleeping next to me snored and whistled through his nose with such virtuosity that I was still listening to him when dawn broke.

Wednesday June 19th

E arly next morning we set off again for Brive. A heavily laden car was in front of us—it was the panicky Belgian fleeing south. After a few kilometres we were forced to stop by an unexpected obstruction: a roadblock manned by *gendarmes*. Only military trucks were being allowed to travel on the main roads in Corrèze, the *département* in which we now were. We would have to turn back and find an alternative road to Brive, which was no easy task. After an hour spent driving up and down the by-roads, our truck finally came to a halt on the outskirts of Lubersac. The miller had a brief confab with his family and decided to settle hereabouts rather than stick to the original plan of going further. So I bid these good folk farewell and set off again on foot.

As I crossed the square at Lubersac, an elderly village policeman was beating loudly on a drum and announcing the latest edict. From today, any evacuation or displacement of refugees within the *département* of Corrèze was forbidden. I continued calmly on my way.

The road twisted and turned upwards. I climbed slowly up the hill, weighed down by my bags and worn out by the stifling heat. The sun was scorching, a real Midi sun. The white surface of the road hurt my eyes. Meadows, hills, groves of chestnut trees, ancient ruins—everything was flooded with light. The cicadas sang, deafeningly.

A huge military truck towing a trailer came up the hill. I waved to the driver, who invited me to climb up onto the running-board, which I managed to do. It was a rather hazardous undertaking, for the running-board was minute and situated at the front, slanting on either side of the truck's pointed beak. There was just enough room to stand on tiptoe. I travelled several kilometres in this fashion, clinging to the nose of this monster as it sped along. The first time it came to a halt, I took the opportunity to climb up onto the elevated back of the trailer. Perched up there, it was like being on the back of an elephant. But I was able to admire at my leisure the beauty of the surrounding countryside.

Suddenly, through the old chestnut trees the Château de Pompadour came into view, with its fat round towers, looking like a typical fairy-tale castle. I fancied I could see flunkeys, page-boys, and scullions running hither and thither in the courtyard, a princess spinning her distaff at the top of a tower, and Puss-in-Boots arriving in a gilded coach. The vision only lasted a second, for the château disappeared from sight at the next turn.

The names of the villages all ended in -ac or -our, showing that we really were in the Languedoc. We passed another château, rising on a rock from the middle of a wood. Haughty if tragic-looking, this one— in ruins, its towers demolished and covered in ivy. Troubadour songs once echoed throughout this region of chivalrous culture, up until the day when the Albigensian Crusade put it to fire and sword. In place of courts of love and tournaments came bonfires of heretics and processions of penitents. The spirit of the Dominican Spain of the Catholic kings triumphed over the probably too liberal spirit of the Counts of Toulouse, who allowed the Bogomil heresy—brought from the East by the Crusaders—to take root here. [1]

What a strange miscarriage of the great expeditions *outremer*[2] was this mysterious thrust to the Levant that we call the Crusades! Despite everything that is usually said, it wasn't simply the covetousness of the lords, greedy for booty, nor the liking for warlike adventure so typical of the feudal world, that made Western Christians leave their homes and possessions to take up the Cross and set off, gripped by an irresistible urge to journey to the unknown lands of the East. Above all, it was one vast pilgrimage, albeit an armed one, a movement that was essentially religious in nature—to which admittedly other motives soon attached themselves. Sometimes a legend which grows

---

[1]The Bogomils were a Gnostic, dualistic sect who believed, among other things, that material creation was intrinsically evil.

[2]Literally 'overseas', but also the collective name for the Crusader states.

up around a lived event, like the poetry it may inspire, reveals the hidden essence of a historical fact, one that those historians who rely solely on so-called "positive" data fail to notice. Men went to the East primarily in order to liberate the Holy Sepulchre. They also went to discover the mysterious country where St John the Apostle lived "eternally", ruling over a Christian people.[3] They went above all because driven by a vague religious restlessness which was later to find expression in the mystical poem entitled the *Queste del Saint Graal*, in which the chalice used at the Last Supper is said to symbolise the fullness of the gifts of the Holy Spirit.[4] However, the Crusades degenerated into a war of pillage and destruction, its participants setting upon Eastern Christians. Instead of the spiritual kingdom of St John, an ephemeral one was established: the Latin Empire. Instead of the Holy Grail, the knights brought back to the West the Manichean heresy of the Bulgarians.[5] This in turn resulted in a new crusade, of the North of France against the Midi. This was the first "war of religion" to bloody French soil. The Languedoc would witness others, 300 years later.[6]

At last, we arrived at Brive-la-Gaillarde. I was surprised to see all the shops open, elegant women in summer outfits, crowds strolling peacefully up and down the streets or sitting at tables on café terraces. Once again, I felt like a fish out of water, a stranger to this tranquil, settled way of life, a vagabond caught up in the adventurous life of the highway. I lost no time in getting out of town. Soon it was far behind me at the foot of the hill, its roofs, steeples and factory chimneys shimmering in the haze of a summer's day.

An elderly peasant who was tending his vines looked up at me as I passed. "Have you come far like that?" he asked. "From Paris," I

---

[3] The allusion is to John 21:23, as read by the crusaders—the belief that "the disciple whom Jesus loved [. . .] should not die".

[4] The first known narrative dealing with the Grail was Chrétien de Troyes' *Le Conte du Graal*, written 1180–1192. The version Lossky here refers to, however, is by a 13th century Cistercian. More ascetic and theological, it is far less concerned with courtly themes.

[5] It was in Bulgaria in the 10th century that the Bogomil heresy began.

[6] The Albigensian Crusade lasted from 1209 to 1229. Roughly "three hundred years later" in the mid-sixteenth century, the *Guerres de religion* between Catholics and Protestants erupted.

replied. "What a mess!" he continued. "Ah, there's no two ways about it, we certainly deserve what's happening to us today! They'll be down here, too, the *Boches*, soon enough . . . Still, got to carry on working just the same. *Allez*, good luck!"

A few kilometres further on, the character of the landscape suddenly changed. The hillsides were no longer green and smiling, but arid and severe. Grass bleached by the sun, a few rocks, a few clumps of brushwood—nothing but a dry, dreary expanse of land for as far as the eye could see. These limestone plateaux—or *causses*, as they are called in Quercy—put me in mind of Spain. You could easily imagine the emaciated silhouette of Don Quixote making his way along such a road with its barren slopes, on his thin mount, followed by his faithful squire. In fact, in a little inn where I was served goat cheese and local sour wine, I did come across Sancho Panza. In the person of a large Spaniard, fat-bellied and jovial, a farmer on his way back from Brive. Instead of a donkey, however, he had an old car. He gave me a lift in it.

I travelled six kilometres with him before having to continue on foot again, making for Turenne. Just then a band of peasants in blue smocks surrounded me, behaving for all the world like *communards*.[7] They were armed with hunting rifles and were clearly *gardes territoriaux*. They had probably mistaken me for a parachutist. "One more step," I was told, "and you'll be arrested! It's forbidden to travel from one commune to another. Go back where you came from!" I became angry. Faced with my fiery eloquence, the "*communards*" had to give in and I went on my way, preparing myself to encounter yet further obstacles before reaching the boundary between the Corrèze and the Lot.

The Château of Turenne could be seen from afar with its square keep and a rounded tower, as could what remained of its tall ramparts—a proud, severe silhouette . . . Proud too, this very name Turenne, sounding like a clarion call from the past. It was a name that

[7]Members and supporters of the short-lived Paris Commune of 1871, when the ordinary population took up arms. Lossky is perhaps reminded of these *communards* since they too were active in the wake of a French defeat at the hands of Germans–or, more precisely, Prussians.

wrung my heart, in a moment of intense anguish.[8] We had had Turenne; there had been Foch, too.[9] There will be other such leaders when the hour comes.[10] For the time being, it is a case of gritting one's teeth and marching straight ahead along the road.

Here comes the latest obstacle: four *gardes territoriaux* at a level-crossing. I get ready to confront them. But just at this moment, a car drives up. All four of them rush at the woman driver, demanding to see her identification papers. And I walk on past them, calmly, without quickening my pace. The departmental boundary-stone states that I am in the Lot, where freedom of movement is still allowed. I am on the final stretch.

I managed to get one last lift for a few kilometres with a couple from a nearby village. Opening the door to let me out, the man said, "You're nearly there. The farm you're making for is only two kilometres from here. It's a country house with a mill, in fact. You'll see it on the right hand side of the main road. You just need to keep walking straight ahead."

The last kilometre—the hardest, perhaps, but also the most heartening. I was simultaneously overwhelmed by the joy of being reunited with my family any minute now, and by fatigue. I felt utterly weary. It was the accumulated weariness of seven days of life on the roads, when it seemed the whole of France was on the move. The joy of arriving and the sadness of having had to leave merged into one, creating in me a new feeling: a serene melancholy at having reached journey's end.

[8]The Vicomte de Turenne (1611–1675), Marshal of France, was an outstanding general who commanded the French forces in the early campaigns of Louis XIV.

[9]Ferdinand Foch (1851–1929), soldier, military theorist and writer, served as General in the French Army during World War I and was made Marshal of France in its final year, 1918. He was chosen as supreme commander of the allied armies, a position that he held until 11 November 1918, when he accepted the German request for an armistice. He advocated peace terms that would make Germany unable ever to pose a threat to France again. His words after the Treaty of Versailles—"This is not a peace. It is an armistice for 20 years"—would prove prophetically accurate.

[10]Prophetic words indeed; for De Gaulle had just made his historic *Appeal* on the BBC, the very evening before.

The very last kilometre! Yes, I was overwhelmed by the immense fatigue of the roads, but the misery I had witnessed weighed heavy on me, too. Hunger and thirst; heat and rain; hope and distress; death by exhaustion and death by violence. The horrors of bombardment and narrow escapes; open country and places of refuge; panic attacks and rash acts of bravery; the collapse of government and empty words; dignified tears and quiet resignation; cruel acts of callousness and small, humane acts of thoughtfulness; moments of solitude and moments of solidarity; the sadness of being on the move and sadness when resting; departures and arrivals; beginnings and endings. I was leaving it behind, all this misery, horror, sadness and magnanimity. Yet I still felt nostalgia for the roads of France. For they had revealed to me the truth of what the King of Wisdom said: "Sadness is better than laughter, for it is by sadness of the face that the heart becomes joyful".[11] They had shown me the treasures of misery and the hope that shines amid the greatest imaginable distress. They had taught me to recognise Providence where we normally only see chance. They had taught me to know that the ways of God are not our ways, although we are called to follow them all the same, as did the saints of old.

"Lord, we shall never be able to follow Your way; it is too steep. We are but poor mortals used to walking our human ways."

"O people of little faith! Have you not understood, as did the saints, the mystery of the Cross, in all its width and length and depth and height?"

"Lord, how can we carry Your Cross? We are weighed down already under our own sorrow. Do you wish our death?"

"Have I not commanded those of you who would come after Me to deny yourselves and take up your cross and follow Me? Would you prefer, in seeking to avoid the cross I am giving you, to lose your life?"

"Lord, we have carried our cross for centuries, but the one You offer us today is too heavy and is beyond our capabilities; for we are a nation grown old from much toiling, worn out by travelling along a road which is too long ."

[11]A free rendering of Proverbs 15:13.

"Will not My uncreated grace be sufficient for you? Have you not learned that My strength is fulfilled in weakness? Or that I choose the weak of the world to confound the strong? That My weakness is greater than men?"

"Lord, You have humiliated us in the sight of the nations by our defeat, by our weakness."

"I have allowed Satan's angel to chastise you so that you might recognise your weakness and let My strength be accomplished in you."

"Lord, why do You wish to chastise France more than other countries?"

"Because I chastise all those whom I love. Take heart then, and repent. Behold, I stand at the door and knock."

"Lord, Your word is hard to hear. Our prelates and spiritual guides never spoke to us like this."

"Leave the dead to bury their dead and follow Me. For you are called to re-establish My Church in western lands. You shall be My Apostles of the Last Times."

The roads of France traverse space and time: *routes nationales*, ancient royal roads, pilgrim roads, Roman roads, roads linking the towns of ancient Gaul. The present merges with the past; the past encroaches upon the present. There is only one France, eternal. Her armies forever march East—armies of 1939, of 1914, of 1870; armies of the Empire, armies of the Revolution, armies of the Kings going down to the Plains of Lombardy in a brilliant cavalcade. Joan of Arc rides across a country at war, making for the Loire to save her king. Aucassin and Nicolette travel the roads, singing their *lais*.[12] Pilgrims

[12]Technically speaking, Lossky should have used the word *laisse* rather than *lai*, "lay". (In fairness, we must remember that this is a Journal, written at speed and never revised for publication by the author himself.) *Laisse* is the term for an assonated strophe—or a group of them—when the context is mediaeval. The early 13th C story of *Aucassin et Nicolette*—perhaps the most charming work of French mediaeval fiction—is the only surviving example of a *chantefable*, the word used in the text to describe itself. It is a mixture of alternating prose and *laisses*, the latter being set to music—hence Lossky's use of the verb "sing". The melody survives in the

make their slow way to lands on whose soil the Apostles walked. Knights still seek the Holy Grail on mysterious, distant roads. The *ost* of Charlemagne returns from Saragossa and Roland's horn can still be heard sounding in the distance at Roncevaux.[13] Townsfolk and villagers, the remnants of routed armies, convoys laden with women and children—all forever flee from invaders: Huns, Saracens, Normans, English . . . Germans.

But at the moment the road is becoming engulfed in darkness, for night draws near. Night is falling on France, on Europe, on the whole world.

Those who, like the wise virgins, have kept their lamps tended will still have light. As for those who have allowed their lamps to go out, let them light them again. Let them seek more oil before it is too late. For the journey through the night will be long.

Saint Geneviève's taper—lit by divine fire [14]—still shines on her hill from time immemorial, in our sombre night-time, too. But our lamps have run out of oil and the wind is blowing out the flickering flame of the candles we hold in our hands.

Will dawn ever break again? The *gallicinium* will be a long time coming.[15] The cocks on the steeples have not yet crowed. And when they do finally broadcast their triumphant cry across the land, what will it signify? A new call to St Peter—as of old, on that other night, when he denied his Lord—a call to reawaken the Church of Rome to

manuscript. This tale of young love thwarted but eventually triumphant manages to parody courtly and other mediaeval conventions in an utterly engaging manner.

[13]*Ost* is the Anglo-Norman word used in *La Chanson de Roland* to mean "host" or "army". Roland—hero of the tale and Charlemagne's nephew—was in command of the rearguard as the army retreated from Spain over the pass of Roncevaux. Despite heroic resistance against the ensuing Saracens, Roland was the last survivor. He himself died from the exertion of blowing his horn in order to recall Charlemagne, who does turn back and is ultimately victorious.

[14]The allusion is to the construction of the first basilica to Saint Denis, done at Geneviève's insistence. When she was visiting the building-site one night with her companions, the wind blew out the taper that was lighting the way of the little group. She took the taper in her own hand, whereupon it promptly relit itself, remaining unaffected by any squall or gust. Icons of St Geneviève typically depict her holding a candle or taper.

[15]*Gallicinium*: cockcrow.

new life? [16] Or will it herald the dawn of the New Day that will have no end?[17] No one can say.

❧

"Our Lady, Queen of Mercy, it was to you that one of our kings entrusted his kingdom for 300 years.[18] This span of time came to an end two years ago. Do not leave us to walk through the night alone.

Our Lady, you whom the children saw crying on the hill at La Salette, since you can no longer withhold the avenging arm of your Son, grant us the strength to carry our cross.

Our Lady of the roads of France, send your Apostles of the Last Times, to rekindle faith, to rout the powers of darkness, to illumine our path through this benighted France and this benighted world."

Roger d'Élan[19]
La Borgne, 24 June–14 July 1940

---

[16]This now reads like a prophetic announcement of Vatican II.

[17]In Orthodox thinking this day is referred to as the Eighth Day—coincidentally but appropriately, one more than Lossky's seven spent on the road.

[18]Louis XIII ("the Just") and Anne of Austria had no male heir; the king's brother was plotting to take over as successor. In 1637, the king therefore placed his kingdom under the protection of the Virgin, in an act known as "Louis XIII's vow". In September 1638, after 23 years of marriage, a son was born: Louis-Dieudonné (literally "gift of God"), the future Louis XIV.

[19]This is the pseudonym on the manuscript. In fact, Élan is simply a translation of *los'* which means "elk" or "moose" in Polish and Russian. (The author's ancestors were Polish until the end of the 18th C, when they became Russian.) The horn of an elk figures on the family coat of arms. The name *Lossky* seems to have been derived from it in the 12th or 13th C. [*Original editor's note.*]

The Human Face
of the Theologian

BY JEAN LOSSKY[1]

L ong before my father died, when I happened to be reading
Shakespeare's *Julius Caesar* for the first time and had got to the
part where Mark Antony delivers the funeral oration in honour
of Brutus, I sensed instinctively and for certain that here was an
appraisal that fitted him—whether alive or dead—probably even
more than Brutus.

> *His life was gentle and the elements*
> *So mixed in him that Nature might stand up*
> *And say to all the world, "This was a man!"* [2]

During the hours immediately following the news of his death, I was
in a state of shock, unable to function normally. Yet it was this quotation which kept coming to mind. More than ever, I was convinced that
it summed him up—him more than anyone I had ever known.

Theologians will remember him for his theological writings; scholars will recall his research into Meister Eckhart. These are matters in
which I am not myself competent to judge. Yet it is no mere filial piety
that occasions the love and admiration that I have for him. Rather,
it is what he resolved to be as a human being and was: "a Man". A

---

[1]This article first appeared the year after Lossky's death in *Contacts*, no. 28,
1959. Jean Lossky, born in 1932, went to America in 1953, served in the US Army
in Korea, obtained American naturalisation, then worked as a cabin interpreter for
the UN in New York and Geneva. Sent on a mission to the Far East, he stopped in
Bali on the way. During his visit of the island, he was killed in a motorcycle accident,
in May 1971.

[2]Act V, scene v.

modern crusader, with perhaps a touch of the Don Quixote about him. Though not in any ridiculous sense. No one who is the first to laugh at himself can be ridiculous. And laugh at himself he certainly did; for there was no trace of vanity in him, nor the slightest pomposity. He laughed at others, too. Throughout his life he managed to retain a childlike quality of mischievousness devoid of malice. The precise sound of his voice may be dying away in the depths of my memory; but his laugh still rings clear in my ears. A full-throated hearty laugh, spontaneous, virile, yet without innuendo.

He sacrificed all his energy—and, in the end, his very life—in the service of his ideals. Yet he was the very opposite of a sectarian. His sense of humour made this an impossibility. Even making allowances for his vast erudition and intelligence, I think—I insist—that, as I knew him, it was his equally acutely developed humour and wit that were the determining factors of his character. The character of a Socrates. Without these two qualities he would have remained a scholar lost in his research, uninterested in the life around him, and himself uninteresting to others except scholars like himself.

However, he was interested in everything—except, perhaps sport and ribaldry. Yet even here he was not uncompromising. If a given sporting spectacle had any aesthetic value, he would appreciate it. If a racy tale were clever, he accepted it as such and collapsed into laughter. After the Bible—which he read from cover to cover every year, trying to live according to its precepts—his favourite reading for a time was Rabelais. Travelling on the métro, he would read Plato in the original; but also and without self-consciousness the adventures of Tintin, which he thoroughly enjoyed.

As for music, his knowledge and understanding was well above average. He collected records, and often went to concerts. He was very interested in art, sculpture and architecture, rarely missing an important exhibition and cycling through the regions of France that he wished to get to know thoroughly. He loved the theatre, whether classical or modern, laughed along with *chansonniers*, and also, it is said, went to the Lido once.[3] Apparently, what particularly

---

[3]The *Lido*, the most legendary of the Paris cabarets, is situated on the Champs-Elysées.

entertained him was a cancan executed with boisterous verve. He must have seen most of the critically acclaimed films made in his day, including *Fanfan la Tulipe*.[4] And Gina Lollobrigida was certainly far from arousing his scorn or disdain.

As is well known, he was profoundly religious and a strict observer of the Church's rites. However, he detested and scoffed at bigotry and was never as funny as when cracking jokes—never cruel ones, be it said—at the expense of clergy or hierarchy. During the Great Fast, he was a real ascetic, though this did not prevent him from thinking of himself, with a certain ingenuousness, as a "bon viveur", a gourmet.

His code of honour was simple. Among his ancestors were knights who had fought in the Crusades and he too wished to be a Knight of the 20th Century. "To demand justice for oneself is to demean oneself," he used to say. "It is for others that we should desire it." He lived and died faithful to this motto.

My father was 54 when he died. Many people think he died too young, without having completed his various research projects, leaving many a book unpublished, many a task not even started. This may be true. Even so, I can say that, rarely if ever, was a life lived more to the full, even by a centenarian. Who amongst us can in all honesty claim that he has never used an expression such as, "I am doing this or that simply to kill time"? My father never did, although he often had good reason to do so. To his mind, the concept of "killing time" was a form of suicide. He detested the very idea of it. He was happy because always interested in whatever it was he was doing. He never lived aimlessly, waiting for better days to turn up. Any free time was filled with a rich inner life, open to the widest range of interests. So he never once let himself be dragged along by events. This would-be knight bestrode his own life resolutely, guiding it with a firm hand. *He* was in charge and knew exactly where he was going. In the true sense of the word, he lived to the full every minute of his life on earth, as can only someone who knows the true meaning of liberty.

To sum up a life so full, so rich that his 54 years seem a century, I can do no better than turn again to Shakespeare's words:

[4]The classic 1952 film, starring Gérard Philipe and Gina Lollobrigida.

His life was gentle and the elements
So mixed in him that Nature might stand up
And say to all the world, "This was a man!"

This was a man. The very paragon of a man, in fact. "*When comes such another?*"[5]

[5]*Julius Caesar*, Act III, scene ii.

The Pilgrim Poet

BY MARIE SÉMON[1]

T he text of *Seven Days*—in which sacred and secular meet and at times even merge—will come as a surprise to those readers familiar only with the author's theological writings. While it is striking to find here the seeds of his later works, what these pages reveal above all is the man himself, in all the rich diversity of his talents.

Splendidly written—on the basis of facts and lived events, and recalling fellow humans encountered on their path of sorrow or on their road to death—*Seven Days* differs from a normal account in the way the author meditates on the most diverse of topics, including the meaning of suffering itself.

Although enamoured of the earth's beauty for its own sake, Vladimir Lossky always goes further, seeking God in His creation—and finding Him. He sees God's image and likeness in the faces of those saints whose memory he brings back to life as he walks across the beautiful land of France. His vast culture—philosophical, historical and literary as much as theological—feeds his rich meditations in a quite natural manner. His keen historical sense has its source in that temporal and spatial awareness that is proper to the poets: he *hears* the voices of the troubadours; at the Château de Pompadour he *sees* the flunkeys, pages and scullions busying themselves as they prepare for Puss-in-Boots's feast. Charles Perrault, traditional children's songs, Aucassin and Nicolette, Péguy: all are celebrated as he walks

[1]Specially written for the original French edition of 1997. Marie Sémon, the elder of Lossky's two daughters, is emeritus Professor of Russian Literature at the University of Paris-Nanterre and a specialist in Tolstoy.

along—with difficulty certainly, risking his life at every moment like his chance companions. Yet, no sooner does he step out than the land's past begins to resonate. Geography becomes history: the secular, but more often than not the sacred, history of *"France la sainte"*.

Moreover, his temporal sensitivity, akin to that of a Christian poet, enables him to see much further than these past events brought to life again. He seems to distinguish, amid the chaos of the exodus from Paris, hope for the future. That epitomised later by the *Résistance*, in which he himself was to take part. In this context, his comments for June 19th are particularly striking, considering that at the time he knew nothing of Général de Gaulle's *Appel* of the previous day. Passing near the Château de Turenne, he evokes the glory of this name "which sounds like a clarion call from the past". "We had Turenne," he adds, "we had Foch, we shall have other great leaders when the hour comes."[2] Was this mere coincidence? No, rather the intuition of a pilgrim poet to whom time and space speak, an intuition that he constantly places in the hands of God and the *Panagia*. Thus, past and future seem to meet up in a present that is rich in foresight.

Those who knew him will recognise in this *Journal* the man himself—his modesty, his nobility, his warm smile, his laugh, his courage coupled with humour. The tragedy of the exodus from Paris is transformed at times into a picaresque adventure, with allusions to the Iliad, the Odyssey and Don Quixote, his favourite hero. Disaster is transfigured, becoming a spiritual feat.

But a work of art—and this is one, however modest—matures over time. Today the "nostalgia for the road" that runs through the entire text like a *leitmotiv*—a road that leads from one holy place to another—reveals Vladimir Lossky to be a "pilgrim of the Absolute".[3] For such he was, throughout his life, to the end walking always in the sight of God, always seeking Him.

---

[2] The *Appeal of 18th June* was delivered by de Gaulle, in his capacity as leader of the newly-formed Free French Forces, from London on the BBC. He declared that the war for France was not yet over, and rallied the country in support of the Résistance. It is one of the most important speeches in French history.

[3] The phrase is from the 1914 book with this title by Léon Bloy.

I had the privilege of being with him as he was dying—so cruelly, as it seemed to us. Yet the very evening before this day that was so terrible for us, I remember that it was death that we had talked about throughout a convivial dinner. The next day, as he came staggering into the apartment, I dragged him along so as to lie him down on the couch. Beside myself, I suggested every kind of medicine I could think of. Each time he shook his head. But when in the end I offered him some holy water from La Salette, he acquiesced. It is, of course, with an invocation to Our Lady of La Salette—"she whom the children saw crying on the hill at La Salette"—that the book ends.

I can still see him, stretched out under the icons, as noble as a prince proved victorious in the toughest of battles, adorned with the chaplet that the Orthodox place on the forehead of the departed.[4] Knight of God! The reflection of eternity on this much loved face had stopped time for us too. We lived from one psalm to the next, each of us reading them continuously at his bedside, as is the custom. "Seek the Lord and His strength; seek His face evermore."[5] As I read aloud these sacred words, it seemed to me that they were my father's last will and testament.

August 1977

---

[4]The reference is to the strip of material that is placed on the brow of the dead person. On it are depicted Christ, Mary and John the Baptist together with the words of the Trisagion, the standard prayer to the Trinity. The dead Orthodox Christian is adorned with this wreath like an athlete who has left the field of contest, or a warrior who has won a victory. The words and figures depicted indicate that the person will receive a crown only through the mercy of the triune God and the mediation of the Mother of God and John the Baptist.

[5]Ps. 105:4, (Septuagint, 104:4.).

The Theologian at Prayer

BY CATHERINE ASLANOFF[1]

> *If you are a theologian, you will pray truly.*
> *And if you pray truly, you are a theologian.*

This dictum of the Church Fathers fits Vladimir Lossky to a tee.[2] Yet, paradoxically, the French saying *la foi du charbonnier*[3] applies to him equally well. For this great theologian, whose intellectual rigour is reflected in his crystal-clear style, had the faith of an innocent child in whose eyes shone the mystery of the Kingdom of Heaven. He may have spoken and written about "the vision of God" but, more so than any of his books, it was his intense gaze that bore witness to his own real vision of God.

A straightforward faith, as unfailing and unshakeable as Vladimir Lossky's, was inevitably forged in the doubts of adolescence—doubts that were overcome during the Russian Revolution. The decisive jolt came when he was present at the trial of Metropolitan Benjamin of Petrograd, one of the first martyrs of the Soviet period and who has now been canonised.[4] The young student found himself caught up in the crowd of faithful who were flocking into the corridors of the law

[1]Specially written for the original French edition. Catherine, the younger of Lossky's two daughters, specialised in catechism, publishing several books with *Les Éditions du Cerf*. She died in May 2000, after a 14-year agonizing struggle against cancer.

[2]Evagrius the Solitary (Pontikos), *On Prayer* § 61.

[3]Literally, the faith of a coalman; the simple faith such as found, especially, among the common people.

[4]Glorified along with other New Martyrs in 1992. Commemorated on Aug. 13 Old Style (July 31 New Style), the date of his execution in 1922.

court to venerate their bishop as he walked, head held high, to the courtroom. As the Metropolitan passed, every one of the believers prostrated themselves to the ground, regardless of the threats of the armed soldiers. This image of a Church in which bishop and flock were united in the blood of martyrdom deeply moved the future theologian.

In November 1922, aged 19, he left Petrograd aboard the so-called "philosophers' ship" that took away the Russian intellectuals expelled by Lenin. Despite this enforced separation, he swore to remain faithful throughout his life to the Russian Church and to its people, guardians of the faith. For, as seen, he had been a direct witness of the first persecutions.

After an absence of 34 years, he was able to return to Russia in 1956. In a letter to his father written in September of that year, he described how he felt on the occasion of his new encounter with the Russian people:

> Suddenly finding myself in Russia again, I was struck by the contrast with the Touraine I had left behind. The landscape struck me at first as being impoverished, gloomy, silent—as did the people. I was yet to discover the strength of their hidden, inner life. Their natural talent—their potential, as it were—for spirituality.
>
> Can one say of the Russians that they are a "God-bearing people"? Or is that too categorical an appraisal, one that is therefore deceptive and devoid of nuances? In any case, it is certainly true that this is a people with an exceptional talent for religion, linked closely to what might be called an acceptance of suffering. It is a characteristic that has nothing in common with the *amor fati* of the Ancients nor with that Hindu detachment that is so ready to submit to the hazards of the Wheel of Destiny. Rather, it is a genuine, positive moral property. In a way, an innate Christianity. (Theologically speaking, this is a clumsy notion, "heretical" perhaps; but I can't find any other way of expressing myself.)
>
> When I left Russia in 1922 at the age of 19, I was profoundly aware of having lost something essential, something fundamental—even though, to tell the truth, I have always been a "Westerniser".

And I understood why, when separated from Russia 34 years earlier, I had felt rejected, deprived of something essential. What in Russia goes without saying—as if almost "natural", most exceptionally during the time of persecution—seems implausible, incomprehensible once one is torn from the roots that bind you to this resigned people, a people that is able to suffer without striking a pose, without reservation, without false modesty.

The fruits of these deep-seated characteristics among those inhabitants of the USSR who haven't lost a human face—and, really, that means the vast majority of them—these fruits are clearly seen in Church, among the faithful. There, Russian "heaviness" is transfigured into a surprising, otherworldly "lightness", as if borne on wings. It is transformed into freely expressed prayer in crowded churches that are bursting at the seams, during the long services—some of them lasting for four hours—but in which one takes part without noticing any fatigue, without one's mind wandering or being distracted by idle thoughts.

There is a prodigious strength in this people at prayer. Time and again I felt ashamed, experiencing a sort of inferiority complex in the presence of these simple, common folk. As for Father Basil Krivocheine,[5] a reserved man—I would even say a dry man (descended as he is, after all, from a family of Petrograd bureaucrats, and normally displaying the ascetic behaviour of an Athonite monk)—he said to me: "I don't know what's come over me. I can't stop weeping during the services". Even now—I saw him just two weeks ago—he can't talk about our experiences without profound emotion.

The evening before we left, a *molieben* for safe travel was served in our honour, in one of the churches in the suburbs of Moscow.[6] As we were leaving the building to get into the waiting

---

[5]The noted Patristic scholar, author of important works on St Gregory Palamas and St Symeon the New Theologian. Later, Archbishop of Brussels and Belgium.

[6]A *molieben* (from Church Slavonic *Mol'ba*—prayer, supplication) is a short liturgical service usually centered on a particular need or occasion: the New Year, a journey, an illness, an act of thanksgiving, etc. It may be addressed to Christ, the Mother of God, or to saints. Its general structure is that of Matins.

cars, the people crowded round us to say their moving farewells. That's another characteristic: the warm, friendly welcome accorded "strangers" recognised as "brothers". The evening sun lit up the golden cupolas, all the bells were ringing out, and *babas* bowed to the very ground. Since our cars kept getting stuck in the ruts, we could hear their voices behind us for a long time: "Adieu, dear friends. Don't forget us! Come and see us again!"

Today, from my adopted country of France—marvellous in its own way, though far from Russia—I look back on my meeting with the Russian people as a precious spiritual experience, as a privilege that I was granted. I could never have lived or worked in Russia, whatever the régime; I am too deeply rooted in the West, in France in particular. Yet here is another Russian characteristic: to be more European than all the other Europeans. Proof of this can be found in the city of Petrograd, in Pushkin, in the culture of the noble classes of the last two centuries, prior to the catastrophe that was the new "Muscovite Russia" with its Asiatic roguery.

Vladimir Lossky's day was structured by the rhythm of his prayer. He never missed saying the set prayers, for example. I remember how—when we were going home from a show or concert or play, late in the evening on the last métro—my father would refuse to sit down, though the train was all but empty. He would stand upright, looking straight ahead, intently. He was saying the Evening Prayers, making discreet signs of the Cross on his chest. Early in the morning, after washing and shaving, he would make a pretext of buying bread for the family to make a long walk along the *quais* of the Seine—from the Île-Saint-Louis to Notre Dame—reciting the Morning Prayers all the while.

Every day he went to his tiny office perched among the rooftops of Paris, overlooking the Church of Saint-Étienne-du-Mont, where Saint Geneviève's tomb is located. He would read the Bible as he walked along, often stopping, even at the risk of getting run over. During his arduous research work—a relentless struggle to make known the negative theology of Meister Eckhart—he would rush down the crooked stairs of the dilapidated Quartier Latin building several times a day, to draw strength from the patron saint of Paris, so venerated by the Lossky family. (We only became aware of this after his death, when told about it by the lady who sold the candles.)

Both our parents prepared for Sundays by attending the long Vigil Service on Saturday evenings.[7] Each Sunday was an event, a celebration of the radiant joy of Christ's Resurrection. Feast days were a high point, when the mystery of salvation was experienced more fully with each passing year, in a spirit of re-discovery and always with a sense of wonder. They were never a mere repetition of past events, but instances of God's revelation and a time to experience a heightened expectation of the Age to come.

My father's life fitted quite naturally into the liturgical cycle; so it is not surprising that the last liturgy at which he went to communion was on the Feast of the Meeting of Our Lord.[8]

Lord, now lettest Thou Thy servant depart in peace, according to Thy word: for mine eyes have seen Thy salvation, which Thou hast prepared before the face of all people: a light to lighten the Gentiles and the glory of Thy people Israel.[9]

That year the feast fell on the Sunday of the Publican and Pharisee.[10] Coming, as it did, immediately prior to his departure from this world, nothing could have been more appropriate. For, like the Publican, he himself was the humblest of men. A true scholar, he toiled meticulously at his research, not as a thankless task but rather as a gift from God. He never spoke in a way that revealed signs of pride concerning the merit of his writings. Everything was from God, to Whom he gave thanks for each inspired thought. He never claimed any of these as his own, but always sought to connect them to the living Tradition of the Church.

[7]In the Russian tradition, a combination of Vespers, Matins and the First Hour.

[8]February 15th Old Style, February 2nd on the civil calendar.

[9]The Song of Symeon is sung, of course, at every Vespers or Vigil service; but more solemnly so on this feast, when Our Lord is brought to the Temple and meets His chosen people in the persons of Simeon the Elder and Anna the Prophetess and when its phraseology informs several of the special texts.

[10]The 2nd of the 5 Sundays which make up the preparatory pre-Lenten cycle.

Not unto us, O Lord, not unto us, but unto Thy name give glory, for Thy mercy, and for Thy truth's sake.[11]

On the Sunday before his burial, the Church read the Parable of the Prodigal Son, a son who returns home.[12] The rich life of Vladimir Lossky, a life full of poetry, was in a sense an illustration of this magnificent text. For the very day before he died, he met up again with his own son Jean, who had left for the United States four years earlier. Chance? No, Providence, rather. Among the last words of this father filled with joy were: "God has granted me to see my son again!"

The date of his death—February 7th—is the day, according to the Julian Calendar, on which the Russian Church celebrates the memory of St Gregory the Theologian, "Bard of the Trinity". Thus, a further "coincidence" of dates united these two theologians in their love of the Triune God.

August 1997

---

[11]Ps. 113:9 (LXX); 115:1 (AV).
[12]The Sunday of the Prodigal Son is the 3rd in the pre-Lenten cycle.

Biographical Note

1903: Born in Göttingen on June 8th New Calendar (May 26th Old Calendar), that year the Monday after Pentecost.[1] His father—the philosopher Nicolas Lossky—was staying in Göttingen at the time on university business. The family is of an ancient, noble lineage of Western origin.

Childhood and adolescence in St. Petersburg. Extremely sensitive as a child, particularly when confronted with the mystery of death. The Socratic presence of his father leaves its mark on him.

1920–1922: Studies at the University of Petrograd, as the revolutionary period is in full swing. Comes under the influence of Lev Karsavin, historian of ideas and philosophy, who draws his attention to the importance of the Fathers and to the dogmatic importance of the *Filioque* question. Becomes interested in the mediaeval history of the West. Like his father, refuses to emigrate.

1922: In November, the Soviet government expels Nicolas Lossky and his family.

1922 (end)—October 1924: In Prague. V.L. works with N.P.Kondakov, specialist in Byzantine art and archaeology. Two facets of his character become clear: he has the attitude and tactics of a mediaeval knight; his profound sensibility turns to God. Becomes fascinated by St Francis of Assisi.[2]

1924 (October): Arrives in Paris.

[1]This Monday is, of course, celebrated as the Feast of the Holy Spirit—appropriately enough, given V.L.'s future emphasis on the third Person of the Trinity and on the importance of the *Filioque* issue.

[2]At the end of an open-air lecture on St Francis given by V.L. in Prague, a bird flew down from a nearby tree and settled by his side.

1924–1927: Studies at the Sorbonne for a *licence libre* (non-teaching degree) in mediaeval history. Becomes a friend of the great mediaevalist Ferdinand Lot who (from **1930** on) allows him to work on the *Bulletin du Cange*.[3] Perhaps more importantly still, discovers the courses given by Étienne Gilson, the great authority on mediaeval philosophy. Passionately interested in the subject, he faithfully attends Gilson's lectures at the Sorbonne and at the Collège de France, both before the war and then just after, until Gilson's departure for Canada in 1950.

All in all, a training in the rigour and precision of western scholarship, allied with the acquisition of a taste for thoroughness and depth.

1925–1926: Becomes friendly with Evgraf Kovalevsky and joins the *Confrérie de Saint-Photius*. Out of this decisive friendship there develops the idea—and the vocation—of bearing witness in the West (more specifically in France) to an Orthodoxy that is resolutely universal and capable of reviving French Christianity's own specific traditions. The *Confrérie* is to be used for this witness. To V.L.'s way of thinking it should constitute a Christian knighthood that would correspond to the quest for the Grail, a quest that he interpreted as being, deep down, a search for Orthodoxy.

1927: Becomes interested in Meister Eckhart and begins to assemble materials for a study of his mysticism.

Monday 4th June 1928: On what is again the Feast of the Holy Spirit, marries Madeleine Schapiro, who will be his unwavering companion in all aspects of his life. They will have 4 children. "I have received nothing but good from my family," V.L. would say at a much later date.

1929: V.L.'s research into Meister Eckhart leads him to study St Thomas Aquinas and, more particularly, St Dionysius the Areopagite, the genuinely Christian character of whose writings he elucidates. In *Archives d'histoire doctrinale et littéraire du MoyenÂge* publishes "La notion des analogies chez Denys le pseudo-Aréopagite".

[3]Also known as *Archivum latinitatis medii aevi*, this focuses on Latin lexicology and semantics from the 6th C to the Renaissance.

1931: Out of canonical strictness, and spiritual certainty that the Church must give witness where she is without having to insist on "normal" conditions, refuses to break with the Russian Church. With the other members of the *Confrérie de Saint-Photius*, thus ensures that one part of the Russian colony in Paris remains faithful to the Patriarchal throne in Moscow.

1935–1936: The Sophiological controversy. V.L. opposes the theological system of Father Sergei Bulgakov, in which he detects the risk of a "Christian pantheism". Writes *Spor o Sofii* (*The Controversy concerning Wisdom*). At the request of Metropolitan Sergei—*locum tenens*, and then guardian, of the Patriarchal throne in Moscow—sends him a report of the debate. Metropolitan Sergei replies immediately by condemning the Sophiology of Father Bulgakov.

Of these painful events, particular attention should be drawn to the following two consequences:

1. The ultimately positive impetus given to V.L.'s theological reflection by the thinking of Father Bulgakov.

Indeed, in a sense, V.L.'s entire theology—focussed as it is on the topic of Uncreated Grace and on the Palamite conception of the Divine Energies—can be seen as an attempt to give expression to Father Bulgakov's basic intuition in a manner that is traditional and fully Orthodox.

2. The deep, respectful friendship that henceforth unites V.L. and the future Patriarch Sergei.

A substantial correspondance develops between the two. In many ways, V.L. can be seen to be a disciple of the Patriarch, especially where his conception of the Church is concerned. The Church—as Patriarch Sergei often stressed—belongs to no nation, is linked to no particular place, but must testify to the fullness of Truth everywhere and to all.

16th June 1936: a Patriarchal decree from Moscow receives into the Orthodox Church a western community having its own rite. V.L., together with the Saint Irenaeus Section of the *Confrérie de Saint-Photius*, played a decisive part in this event.

1939: Becomes aquainted with the philosopher Jean Wahl.[4] V.L. the "polemicist" also becomes more and more a man of reflective thought, though one who is profoundly religious.

1940: As France falls to the Germans, attempts in vain to enlist in the army. (He had obtained French citizenship in 1938.) The experiences and reflections occasioned by this attempt form the subject of the present book. In the summer and the autumn, translates the conversation of Saint Seraphim of Sarov on the aim of the Christian life.[5]

As the tragic events unfold, the twin poles of V.L.'s destiny become ever clearer: France, and Orthodoxy.

1940–1944: Takes part in the Résistance, but for him this period is above all a time of further reflection and of bearing witness. At the home of Marcel Moré, participates in regular meetings at which theologians of all denominations, as well as philosophers, discuss such issues as eschatology and transcendance. In 1944 gives a series of lectures on Orthodox mystical theology. These are published the same year as *Essai sur la théologie mystique de l'Église d'Orient*.

1945: Foundation of the *Institut Saint-Denis*, to provide Orthodox theological instruction in French and to train priests for French Orthodoxy.[6] V.L. is Dean of the Institute and teaches Dogmatic Theology and Church History.

The discussions held at Marcel Moré's result in the founding of a periodical entitled *Dieu vivant*. V.L. is a member of the editorial board and, between 1945 and 1948, publishes important articles in this journal.[7]

---

[4]Jean Wahl (†1974), professor at the Sorbonne, was one of the first to introduce Hegel and Kierkegaard to a wider French audience. A supporter of Personalism and Christian Existentialism, he was an effective critic of Sartre and Camus for their denial of a religious dimension to experience.

[5]The reference is to the (now famous) outdoor conversation with Motovilov, in the snow (November 1831). St Seraphim impresses upon Motovilov that the true aim of the Christian life is the acquisition of the Holy Spirit.

[6]At the time, the courses at the *Institut Saint-Serge* were entirely in Russian.

[7]The review ceased publication in 1955. Lossky's articles are reprinted in the posthumous collection entitled *In the Image and Likeness of God*.

In the same year, becomes a research fellow at the *Centre national de recherche scientifique* [founded just before the war, in 1939], and resumes his work on Meister Eckhart.

1945–1946: At the *École pratique des hautes etudes*, gives a series of lectures on the Vision of God in Patristic and Byzantine theology.[8]

August 1947: Receives an invitation—the first of many—to take part in the Summer Conference of the Anglican-Orthodox Fellowship of Saint Alban and Saint Sergius, at Abingdon.

October 1947: Oxford. Takes part in an interdenominational symposium on the theme of the *Filioque*. The Roman Catholic speaker, Fr Henry, is forced—after a lengthy disputation—to admit that a fundamental issue is indeed at stake. One that, for Catholics and Orthodox alike, poses a genuine question of faith.

1952: In collaboration with Leonid Ouspensky, publishes (in German and English) *The Meaning of Icons*. This book contains the article in which he discusses in masterly fashion the notion of Tradition, as opposed to traditions.[9]

1953: Fr Evgraf Kovalevsky breaks with the Moscow Patriarchate and thus compromises, in removing its canonical basis, an important branch of Orthodox witness in France.[10] For V.L. this proves to be an extremely distressing ordeal, one that results in his leaving the *Institut Saint-Denis*. He reacts by becoming more withdrawn. The scholarly and spiritual side of the man prevail definitively over the polemicist. His witness will henceforth be given at the heart of western scholarship and thought.

His activity extends simultaneously to several spheres:

1. **Theological teaching**. Resumes his course on dogmatic and comparative theology in the framework of pastoral courses organised by the Exarchate of the Russian Patriarch.

---

[8]Published in book form posthumously (1962, English translation 1963).
[9]Reproduced in *In the Image and Likeness*.
[10]He had been ordained in 1937.

2. **Academic research.** Builds up his thesis on Meister Eckhart, exploring the western Middle Ages from within, with a level of understanding that benefits both from his own intellectual rigour and the secret illumination of the Holy Spirit.

3. **Ecumenical witness.** Year by year, summer after summer, his witness at the conferences of the Anglican-Orthodox Fellowship of Saint Alban and Saint Sergius becomes ever more central. Several young Anglican theologians become, not merely his friends but his disciples, undertaking a translation of *La théologie mystique de l'Église d'Orient*.

4. **Present at the heart of evolving ideas, as a creative theologian.** Regularly participates in the conferences organised by the *Collège philosophique* under the direction of Jean Wahl, as a listener but also as a speaker.[11] The subjects of his own lectures are:

"Darkness and Light in the Knowledge of God"
"Apophasis and Trinitarian Theology"
"The Theological Notion of the Human Person"
"The Theology of the Image"
"La rose et l'abîme" (on the notion of created being in the thought of Meister Eckhart)[12]

1954 (September): Takes part in the *Congrès international augustinien* in Paris.[13]

1955 (September): Takes part in the second *International Conference on Patristic Studies* at Oxford.[14]

---

[11]The Collège was founded by Jean Wahl in January 1947. His idea was to create a forum for intellectual non-conformism. For many years it was the Collège, not the Sorbonne, that was the truly vital and creative centre of French intellectual life. Lectures for the general public, new research, and new avenues of thought could be sampled—ideas that did not fit into the mould of the universities or the major journals. It survived in its original form until 1974.

[12]So far untranslated into English. The first four lectures appeared in *In the Image and Likeness.*

[13]His paper was entitled "Les elements de 'Théologie négative' dans la pensée de saint Augustin".

[14]He spoke on "Le problème de la 'Vision face à face' et la Tradition patristique

1956 (**August**): Is invited to Russia by the Patriarchate and visits Moscow, Vladimir, Leningrad and Kiev. Experiences the Russian Church at prayer. His involuntary exile is understood as having been providential. Orthodoxy is universal and integrates East and West, thought and life. The theologian becomes fully aware of his roots.

1958 (**7th February**). Dies quickly and easily.

de Byzance". (Eng. tr. by T.E.Bird in Greek *Orthodox Theological Review* 2, Fall 1972, 231–254.)

New Preface to Vladimir Lossky's The Mystical Theology of the Eastern Church

BY FR NICHOLAS LOSSKY[1]

Vladimir Lossky's *Essai sur la théologie mystique de l'Église d'Orient* was first published in 1944.[2] The circumstances of its composition are interesting and worth mentioning. However, for a proper understanding of them, we must go back quite far in Lossky's biography.

Elder son of Nicolai Onufriyevich Lossky (1870–1965), Professor of Philosophy at the University of St Petersburg, Vladimir was born in 1903 in Göttingen where his father was temporarily staying on university business. While still very young, thanks to his French governess, he developed a deep love of France, especially of its mediaeval knightly culture. He was also very attached to his Carolingian ancestors, who became Polish at the beginning of the 13th Century, then Russian at the end of the 18th. It was only at that time that the Losskys became Orthodox. Vladimir's paternal grandmother was still a Catholic. In short, from his earliest days, he had dreamed of going to live in Paris.

---

[1]The translator is grateful to Fr Nicolas Lossky for making available the original French version of this text (the Preface to a recent reprint of the Spanish translation of *Essai sur la théologie mystique*) and for suggesting its inclusion in the present volume. Footnotes are by the translator.

[2]The English translation—*The Mystical Theology of the Eastern Church*—was first published in 1957 by James Clarke & Co Ltd.

In 1922, the family was expelled from Russia by Lenin on the famous "philosophers' ship". Vladimir was 19 at the time, but had already spent two years as a student at the University of Petrograd, as the city was then called, where he had been studying the French Middle Ages. One of his lecturers had introduced him to western philosophers and theologians, most notably Meister Eckhart. Another— L.P.Karsavin, a friend of the family—had interested him at the same time in the Greek Church Fathers. The family stayed for a short while in Berlin, like many other expelled Russians, before settling in Prague, where Vladimir attended the famous Seminar of N.P.Kondakov.[3]

In 1924 he obtained a grant that enabled him, at last, to go to Paris and to enrol at the Sorbonne, where he studied with the great mediaevalist Ferdinand Lot. This led him in turn to become a faithful disciple of the great specialist in mediaeval philosophy Étienne Gilson, at whose feet he got to know personally several Catholic theologians who were themselves disciples of the Master. Among them were Fathers Jean Daniélou, Henri de Lubac, and Yves Marie Congar—all later to become Cardinals—as well as several Protestants and philosophers such as Jean Wahl. It was this group of friends who in 1944 asked Vladimir Lossky to give a series of twelve lectures on the nature of Orthodoxy; for, they explained, everything that they knew about it they owed essentially to the writings of Father Martin Jugie, whose presentation was rather negative, if not to say something of a caricature. It was these twelve lectures that were published, that same year, by Aubier-Montaigne as *Essai sur la théologie mystique de l'Église d'Orient*.

Immediately, the book achieved considerable success. I have often been told by Professors in Catholic seminaries that they recommended it to their students—as an initiation into theology in general, not specifically Orthodox theology! Prior to Vatican II, they would tell me this secretly, taking me to one side so as not to be overheard by their colleagues. It must also be said that it was the same Catholic friends mentioned earlier who, discreetly and obviously without knowing it, prepared the way for the explosion that was the Second Vatican Council. They could hardly have foreseen that one day, without warn-

[3]The Seminar was mainly devoted to Byzantine studies.

ing, the saintly Pope John XXIII would suddenly exclaim, "We must hold a Council!" (This information was conveyed to me by someone who had been his secretary.) As for Vladimir Lossky, he died on February 7th 1958 and so did not live to see this Council, of which he would have heartily approved.

With regard to his book, the first thing worthy of our attention is the very title, with its two expressions: "Mystical Theology" and "Eastern Church". If one reads the first chapter carefully, it becomes apparent that these two notions are qualified, invested with a specific meaning. As for the first—"Mystical Theology"—we must remember that Lossky was writing at a time when, for the majority of his western audience, mysticism was associated only with certain "mystics", exceptional men or women gifted with a very special experience of God. Lossky, however, interprets mysticism quite differently, forcefully stressing that all theology worthy of the name is necessarily *mystical* since it deals with the *mystery* that is God. Like Saint Gregory of Nazianzus (or Gregory the Theologian, as he is known in the Orthodox Church), one of his favourite Fathers, Lossky confesses a God who cannot be "grasped" by the intelligence or by concepts. These themselves, as he used to say, must be deconceptualised. It is this "deconceptualisation of concepts" which leads man to contemplate God as an unfathomable Mystery inaccessible to the human intellect.

The second expression—"Eastern Church"—must likewise be understood aright. In fact, for Lossky, Orthodoxy—in the non-confessional sense of the word, I would add—is neither eastern nor western. It is universal. It is "eastern" or "oriental" only in the sense that, in the East as in the West, in the North as in the South, it is the faithful contemplation of the "Orient from on high", the *Oriens ab alto*.[4] Lossky spent his life seeking out this Orthodoxy, in one form or another, in theologians of the West. It was no accident that his doctoral thesis—completed almost the very day of his death and for which his Director of Studies had been Maurice de Gandillac—was entitled *Théologie négative et connaissance de Dieu chez Maître Eckhart*.[5] It was published posthumously by Vrin in 1960, the Preface

[4]Cf. Zechariah 6:12 (Septuagint); Luke 1:78.
[5]Among the many books produced by M. de Gandillac in his long life, mention

being by Étienne Gilson.[6] As a good disciple of the latter, Lossky admired Thomas Aquinas, while being critical of those of his opinions that are inadmissible for Orthodoxy (for example, the procession of the Holy Spirit understood as being "from the Father and the Son, *tamquam ab uno principio*"). He was equally attached to St Augustine[7] and believed it would probably be possible to demonstrate that he was not a proponent of the *Filioque*. (Cf. "The Procession of the Holy Spirit in Orthodox Trinitarian Doctrine".[8]) He felt that, to this end, an in-depth study of *De Trinitate* ought to be made, something that—dying aged 54—he did not have the time to tackle. Having myself had to undertake such a study in relation to my own research, I can state that his intuition was correct, just as it was for the Spanish councils of the first millennium.

That Vladimir Lossky should have looked for elements of negative theology in the writings of western theologians is linked to the fact that his own theology, as already suggested, was characterised by the negative, or apophatic, approach. However, one should not imagine—as certain people seem to do—that in his case apophatic theology remained something closed in on itself; that is to say, something self-perpetuating and without issue, as in certain non-Christian oriental religions. On the contrary, with him it is a method of thought which results in a theology that can justifiably be styled positive or

must be made of his translation of pseudo-Dionysius (Œuvres complètes du pseudo-Denys l'Aréopagite), published by Aubier in 1943. It is from this translation that Lossky quotes in *Essai sur la théologie mystique*. Lossky had himself already published two articles on Dionysius (one while still in Prague), being especially interested in his "negative" theology. In connection with Father Nicholas' comments on the title of his father's book, it is worth reminding ourselves that one of Dionysius' own works was entitled *Mystical Theology*.

[6]Gilson was a noted specialist in mediaeval philosophy, of which subject he occupied the Chair at the Collège de France. He was elected member of the Académie in 1946.

[7]See his article "Les éléments de 'Théologie négative' dans la pensée de saint Augustin" in *Augustinus Magister*, Vol. 1, (Communications et Actes du Congrès International Augustin, Paris 1954), Éditions des Études Augustiniennes, pp. 575–581.

[8]This article became Chapter 4 of *In the Image and Likeness of God*. (See note 6.)

cataphatic, in the sense that it leads to the contemplation of the Divine mystery that is above and beyond all concepts, to the vision of God, to union with God. As already pointed out, this is why it can be called "mystical theology". It is with good reason that Chapter 2 of the book is entitled "The Divine Darkness" and deals with Dionysius the Areopagite, someone whose writings Lossky studied closely.

The importance and success of the book is further witnessed to by the fact that the Dominicans who run Les Éditions du Cerf have had to re-issue it twice: once in *livre de poche* format in 1990 (an edition which quickly sold out); and again in 2005 in the collection *Patrimoines: Orthodoxie*. The latter contains an excellent Preface by Saulius Rumsas, a young Dominican of Baltic origin, in which he underlines the contribution made by the book to Roman Catholic theology. The same young Dominican has written a very fine text—which he modestly styles a "Foreword"—to introduce another reissue of one of Vladimir Lossky's books. This is the collection of lectures, articles and various other texts that he had assembled for eventual publication in book form—a project that only came to fruition in 1967, thus posthumously. Les Éditions du Cerf purchased the rights from Aubier-Montaigne and republished the book in 2006, also in the series *Patrimoines: Orthodoxie*. It is one that well represents the development of Lossky's thought up to 1957, the year prior to his death. He had chosen the title himself: *À l'image et à la ressemblance de Dieu.*[9]

We owe an enormous debt of gratitude to Father Saulius Rumsas—not simply for the exceptional quality of his Preface and Foreward—but also for the indexes, the footnotes and the bibliographies, which he has updated on the basis of publications (particularly of the Fathers) that appeared between 1944 and 1958. Personally, I am pleased to see that, like myself, Father Saulius considers that Vladimir Lossky—who was not only my father but also my teacher of Dogmatic Theology and Church History—in no way separates the work of the Son from the work of the Spirit. It is true that *The Mystical Theology* contains two separate chapters entitled respectively "The Economy of the Son" and "The Economy of the Holy Spirit", which might

[9]Translated as *In the Image and Likeness of God*, St Vladimir's Seminary Press, 1974.

lead one to overlook the fact that there is a single divine Economy. This possibility is something that Father Georges Florovsky and Metropolitan John (Zizioulas) of Pergamon have rightly criticised. However, the existence of two separate chapters is explained by the historical context in which the book came into being and by the audience to which the original twelve lectures were addressed. At the time, Roman Catholic theology had somewhat glossed over the role of the Holy Spirit in the economy of salvation. Indeed, it was only as a result of his oratorical jousts with my father—conducted amicably out of mutual respect—that Father Yves Congar wrote his great trilogy dealing with the Holy Spirit.[10]

What strikes one in the above two chapters is that Lossky's Christology is, in fact, entirely pneumatological, and his pneumatology entirely Christological. Everything that is written is extremely close to what Metropolitan John (Zizioulas) himself says. To realise this, it is sufficient to reread the important paper the Metropolitan gave during the plenary session of the Fifth World Conference on Faith and Order (1993), held in Santiago de Compostela with the theme "Towards Koinonia in Faith, Life and Witness".[11]

[10]The three volumes were published by Les Éditions du Cerf between 1979 and 1980 and, in a translation by David Smith, between 1983 and 1984 (G. Chapman, London/Seabury Press, N.Y.). It is the last of these that Fr Nicholas is thinking of in particular, for it deals with the history of the doctrine of the Holy Spirit in East and West, and with the position of the Holy Spirit within the Trinity. In 1995 the three volumes were republished as one, entitled *Je crois en l'Esprit-Saint*. The English editions were likewise combined into one: *I Believe in the Holy Spirit*. (Crossroad Publishing Company, N.Y., 1997).

[11]It seems to this reader of *The Mystical Theology* that the above criticism stems from a selective reading and is an artificial construct. For does not Lossky insist that "the work of Christ and the Holy Spirit are [. . .] *inseparable*" (p.167) ? Does he not stress that "the Son and the Holy Spirit accomplish the *same* work on earth" (p. 174)? He may indeed refer, for explanatory purposes, to a "*two-fold* divine economy" (p.156); but, when understood in context, such language to refer to the Son and the Holy Spirit is surely no more suspect than Irenaeus' phrase, the "*two* hands of God" (quoted by Lossky on p.100). Finally, if one is to criticise Lossky on this point, how can St Gregory the Theologian himself escape censure? He who said (Oration 41.5, on Pentecost) that with the Ascension "the works of Christ in the flesh are ended" and that from Pentecost "the work of the Spirit is beginning."

As for Vladimir Lossky's conception of the Church, fully to understand this we must once again go back in time. To the 1920s. In those days, certain members of the Russian emigration had not, in a manner of speaking, unpacked their cases. They fully expected the Bolshevik régime to fall at any time with the result that they could return to Russia and govern her again. Others—and Lossky was of their number—believed that their uprooting was no mere accident of history, but had a providential meaning in the sense that God was expecting something to come out of this presence "in a strange land".[12] This relatively small group asked themselves two questions. Firstly, is Orthodoxy necessarily bound up with a secular "Orthodox" territory, language or culture? If so, it would be necessary to preserve the customs of the country of origin and to live in a sort of Orthodox ghetto. But if not, and if Orthodoxy is not necessarily Russian, Greek, Serbian, Bulgarian, Arab or Romanian, then it is universal. From this follows the second question. What exactly *is* Orthodoxy? To this, the best reply was given by Father Sergius Bulgakov in his book *L'Orthodoxie* (1935).[13] It begins as follows: "Orthodoxy is the Church of Christ on earth". At this point a non-Orthodox might feel inclined to close the book, concluding that it had nothing to say to him. Yet with the second sentence everything changes. "The Church of Christ is not an institution; it is a new life with Christ and in Christ, guided by the Holy Spirit".[14] "To the glory," one is tempted to add, "of the Father." At once, it becomes apparent that Orthodoxy is linked to no particular culture, but has the power to "enchurch" any culture whatever.

In the eyes of the group of young Russians to which Vladimir Lossky belonged, France was an ancient Christian land that for more than a thousand years had been perfectly Orthodox. Thus they sought to learn about French saints who had lived before the schism but also—in Lossky's case—those who had lived after it, such as St Francis of Assisi, St Bernard of Clairvaux, St Joan of Arc, the two Thérèses (the "big" one and the "little" one, as he used to say), as well as many

[12]Cf. Ps. 136:5 (LXX).

[13]Translated as *The Orthodox Church* by Elizabeth S. Cram, edited by Donald A. Lowrie, Centenary Press, 1935.

[14]*Ibid.*, p.9.

others. It was no accident that our parish, founded in 1936, was dedicated jointly to Our Lady Joy of All Who Sorrow and to St Geneviève, Patron of Paris. Lossky's office was located next to the church of Saint Étienne du Mont where St Geneviève's tomb is to be found. Until the day of his death, he prayed daily at it before settling down to his research—research that essentially focussed on Meister Eckhart, the Rhineland mystic in whose writings, as has already been said, he sought out elements of Orthodoxy.

This quest for an Orthodoxy common to East and to West was not, however, limited to the past. If one reads *The Mystical Theology* carefully, one cannot fail to discover passages where the author stresses that which is common to the so-called "oriental" tradition and that to which he was inviting his readers (originally, of course, his listeners) to return: namely, a universal Orthodox tradition. Not for nothing did the Jesuit Father Jean Daniélou come to our home so often to discuss theology with my father. Nor was it accidental that the very first title in the series *Sources Chrétiennes* (of which he was one of the founding editors) was Fr Daniélou's translation and critical edition of St Gregory of Nyssa's *La vie de Moïse*. This appeared in 1942, in French only since the means to produce a bi-lingual edition were lacking during the Occupation. (I still possess a copy of this edition.) Gregory of Nyssa was also the subject of Father Daniélou's Doctoral thesis of 1944. It is of interest to note that, in it, he points out that the *distinction-identité*[15] between the unknowable *essence* of God and the *energies* by which He makes it possible for us to become partakers of His divine nature (Cf. 2 Pt 1:4) is already to be found in Saint Gregory of Nyssa. Jugie had maintained that this distinction was a fourteenth-century "invention" of Saint Gregory Palamas.

Under Jugie's influence, the name Palamas and the term "Palamism" had become so obnoxious for many western theologians

[15]This antinomical expression, coined by Vladimir Lossky, is to be found on p.139 of *Essai sur la théologie mystique de l'Église d'Orient*, originally in the context of a discussion of the *two* natures and the *one* person of Christ. *Identité* here means "identicalness, sameness". In the English version (p. 143), the hyphen has unfortunately been replaced by a dash, which weakens the impact and (at least initially) confuses the reader.

that when, in 1945, Lossky participated with his Catholic friends in founding the review *Dieu vivant*, the article he contributed for the first number was diplomatically entitled "La Théologie de la lumière chez Saint Grégoire de Thessalonique" so as not to cause offence. By 1967, when it was included in *À l'image et à la resemblance de Dieu*, it was renamed "La Théologie de la lumière chez Saint Grégoire Palamas". Since then, things have changed considerably. Several Catholic theologians—and important ones at that—have written about Palamas, taking him entirely seriously. For example, the late André de Halleux.[16] Palamism had been one of the subjects expounded by Lossky in the course of lectures he gave at the Sorbonne from 1945 to 1946. These were published posthumously in Switzerland in 1962 as a book entitled *Vision de Dieu*, long out of print.[17] The Preface was by Father John Meyendorff of blessed memory, himself a great specialist in Saint Gregory Palamas.

At this point, I feel I should touch upon a rather painful business. In 1936, at the request of Metropolitan Sergius (then *locum tenens*, but elected Patriarch of Moscow in 1943), Vladimir Lossky had drawn up a critique of certain aspects of Father Sergius Bulgakov's sophiology. The Moscow Patriarchate then issued a condemnation of these aspects. At the time, Lossky was President of an Orthodox Confraternity, the *Confrérie de Saint-Photius*, and his fellow members practically forced him to publish his critical text. This he was loath to do, not just because Father Sergius was a close friend of the family but because, as Lossky insisted, any critical text placed in the public domain should be ultimately positive, not simply negative. To us, his students, he insisted that Father Sergius was without doubt the greatest Orthodox theologian of the 20th Century and that his sophiology deserved to be corrected so as to render it entirely admissible. However, the members of the *Confrérie* were adamant that his criticisms should be published (in Russian) as a booklet with the title *Spor o Sofii* (*The Controversy concerning Wisdom*). My father was compelled to

[16]A. de Halleux was Professor at the Catholic University of Louvain, and a noted Patristic and Syriac specialist.

[17]Translated as *The Vision of God* by Asheleigh Moorhouse, The Faith Press, 1963.

go along with this decision. Needless to say, this publication provoked a violent quarrel between certain theologians of the *Institut Saint Serge* (of which Father Sergius was Dean) and the *Confrérie de Saint-Photius*. Later, Father Sergius and Vladimir Lossky were reconciled. The entire affair is related in detail in the Memoirs of my grandfather, Nicolai Onufriyevich Lossky, published in Germany but now out of print.[18] The details of this sad affair deserved to be set down, for even today certain people still accuse Vladimir Lossky of having initiated a "denunciation" of Father Bulgakov, close friend of my grandfather.

After this painful parenthesis, let us return to matters more edifying: to further consideration of Lossky's ecclesiology. An important aspect of this is to be found in *In the Image and Likeness of God*, in two adjoining chapters which complement each other—"Concerning the Third Mark of the Church: Catholicity", and "Catholic Consciousness: Anthropological Implications of the Dogma of the Church".

The first—originally published in *Dieu vivant* (No. 10) in 1948—seeks to define the true meaning of "catholicity", and to mark a distinction between it and mere "universality". The etymology of the word—καθ᾿ ὅλον, "according to the fullness", i.e. of Truth, a full reception of Revelation—essentially implies absolute unity amid absolute diversity, two absolutes in the image of the Trinity. The Church is "catholic" insofar as She is the Church of Christ and the Church of the Holy Spirit, "the two hands of the Father", as Saint Irenaeus puts it. In other words, the Church is authentically "catholic" insofar as She is truly "in the image of the Holy Trinity, one in diversity and diverse in unity", to paraphrase Saint Gregory the Theologian.

In the second of the above two chapters we find an interesting clarification of the notion of "consciousness" as it should be understood in the context of catholicity. It relates to the equal dignity of all the baptised. This "equal dignity" in no way abolishes the distinction between the episcopate, the different ordained ministries, and the laity. As Vladimir Lossky often said—he who protested against excessive use of either/or reasoning and who coined, as seen, the phrase *dis-*

---

[18]N.O.Lossky, *Vospominaniya: zhizn'i filosofskii put'*, (Memoirs: a Philosopher's Journey through Life) Wilhelm Fink Verlag, München 1968.

tinction-identité—to distinguish does not always mean to separate or to oppose.[19] Thus it is good to remind ourselves, as Metropolitan John (Zizioulas) often does, that, although bishops are important, they are not *above* the Church. Rather, they are *within* it, themselves being members of the *laos*, the People of God. As Father Jean Tillard says, that is what we mean by *communion*.[20] We should add that for Metropolitan John the bishop is inseparable from his community, to such an extent that a bishop without a community is not really a bishop. As I myself have often written and said, a bishop without a community is not a head, but a skull. Equally, if a bishop and his community are a "body"—the Body of the Church—a community without an *episkopos* (an "overseer") is not a body, but a skeleton. In fact, as Father Tillard stresses, "It is when *taken as a whole* that the Church is the Body of Christ".[21]

If all the baptised are members of the Body of Christ, it becomes obvious—or at least should so become—that none of them is a passive member. Whatever their function, all are members of one another. As St Paul says, "the body is one, [yet] has many members", all of whom need each other (Cf. 1 Cor.12:12). Thus in this communion there is unity in diversity. Which leads us to the point Lossky sought to develop in an article first published posthumously in *Contacts* in 1963[22], but which became the second of the two chapters referred to above: "Catholic Consciousness". He demonstrates that "consciousness", in the context of the Church as Body of Christ, has nothing to do with psychological, philosophical, moral, political or any such kind of consciousness. Nor is it the same as individual consciousness, for in the unity of the Church as Body of Christ, there is no place for individualism, as Metropolitan John (Zizioulas) often reminds us. Every individual member of the Body of Christ is called to become a "person"; that is to say, a being in communion, in the image of the Three Persons of the Holy Trinity, prototype of what humanity in the Church should be.

[19]As, for example, on p.142 of *In the Image and Likeness of God*.
[20]Cf. Jean Tillard, o.p., *L'Église locale* (Cerf 1995).
[21]*Ibid.*, p.149.
[22]*Contacts*, No.42 (1963).

It is a matter, then, of absolute diversity in a unity no less absolute. It seems necessary to put it this way, for if one simply says "unity in diversity", there is the temptation to "explain" the Trinity in terms that tend towards *essentialism*. If, on the other hand, one says "diversity in unity", one risks falling into a form of *personalism*. Now, it is obvious that no philosophical theory can be used to "explain" the Trinity. These two absolutes—unity and diversity—are a paradox inadmissible in philosophy, as was made clear by Saint Gregory the Theologian. (And he knew well enough what philosophy was, having studied it at Athens with his friend Saint Basil of Caesarea.) They are absolutes that amount to a "crucifixion" of the intellect, one that is nonetheless necessary if one is to "deconceptualise all concepts" (to use Vladimir Lossky's expression again) so as to contemplate the mystery, while respecting it as mystery.

In analysing "catholic consciousness", Lossky again makes use of the notion of *distinction-identité*, this time with specific reference to the Economy of the Son and that of the Holy Spirit. As already mentioned, several theologians—in particular, Metropolitan John (Zizioulas)—have reproached him for advocating, as they see it, a "double Economy". There is only, of course, a single divine Economy. Moreover, though one might argue that Vladimir Lossky's expression *distinction-identité* is itself open to criticism, one should not overlook the fact that he goes on to explain that "Both dispensations—of the Son and of the Spirit—are inseparable; they mutually condition one another since one without the other is unthinkable". "One cannot," he continues, "receive the Holy Spirit without being a member of the Body of Christ; one cannot call Christ 'Lord', i.e. have a consciousness of His divinity, other than by the Holy Spirit. Personal multiplicity is crowned by the Holy Spirit only in the unity of the Body of Christ; but it acquires participation in this divinity through the grace conferred virtually upon each one in the gift of the Holy Spirit. This is why the two sacraments of Christian initiation, baptism and chrismation, are so intimately linked."[23] We note once again that for

---

[23] "Catholic Consciousness: Anthropological Implications of the Dogma of the Church", *In the Image and Likeness of God*, p.190.

Vladimir Lossky Christology cannot fail to be pneumatological, nor pneumatology Christological.

In realising this, we discover an essential aspect of what Lossky understands by "catholic consciousness". It belongs to each member of the Church, the Body of Christ; it belongs to each baptised Christian, whether he be bishop or layman. Each is responsible for the whole Church. In short, each member is called to acquire a consciousness that is "ecclesial", a consciousness of what the Church is. Thus, a situation may arise in which a layman feels compelled to tell his bishop that he is at variance with the truth of Orthodoxy. It would indeed be his duty to do so. Conversely, one may not leave one's bishop unless he falls into heresy and persists in it.

Many other theological topics could be mentioned insofar as they relate to Vladimir Lossky's theology, but there is one that cannot be ignored: namely, this great theologian's thoughts concerning the notion of "tradition". In 1952 he wrote a lengthy essay on this very topic for a book entitled *The Meaning of Icons*. Written in collaboration with Leonid Ouspensky, the famous iconographer, it was published that same year in German and English, though the French edition only appeared in 2003.[24] The essay in question is entitled "Tradition and Traditions".

This very important text—which was also included in *In the Image and Likeness of God*—is not unconnected with what was said above concerning the catholic consciousness of each member of the Church, called to become a "person", transcending his individuality so as to be in communion with Christ and with all.

Having discussed, and risen above, the controversy over the distinction, even opposition, between Scripture and Tradition that raged during the Reformation and the Counter-Reformation, Vladimir Lossky seeks to define the true meaning of Tradition. For him, "tradition" with a small 't' is something of secondary importance, something that may change from place to place, from age to age, according

---

[24]*Le Sens des icônes* (Les Éditions du Cerf, 2003).

to local needs and the challenges of history and geography. All this he styled the "horizontal line" of Church history. In the final analysis, Tradition with a capital T is what each baptised person receives when chrismated: "the seal of the gift of the Holy Spirit". In other words, it is nothing less than the breath of the Holy Spirit within the Church, incorporating us into the Body of Christ, with Whom He is the "criterion" of Truth. Lossky goes so far as to say that Tradition (understood in this sense) constitutes the "critical Spirit" of the Church, one that enables errors to be corrected wherever they appear. This is, in fact, one of his richest theological insights.

In conclusion, I would add that—like many of the ideas contained in the posthumous publication *In the Image and Likeness of God*—it is one that is already present, if less developed, in Vladimir Lossky's classic: *The Mystical Theology of the Eastern Church*.